KDE Application Development

Uwe Thiem

MACMILLAN
TECHNICAL
PUBLISHING
U•S•A

KDE Application Development

By Uwe Thiem

Translated from KDE Programmierung/ Uwe Thiem
(Franzis' Verlag 1999)

English translation version:

International Standard Book Number: 1-57870-201-1

Library of Congress Catalog Card Number: 99-65424

Printed in the United States of America

First Printing: December, 1999

03 02 01 00 99 7 6 5 4 3 2 1

Interpretation of the printing code: The rightmost double-digit number is the year of the book's printing; the rightmost single-digit number is the number of the book's printing. For example, the printing code 99-1 shows that the first printing of the book occurred in 1999.

Trademarks

Warning and Disclaimer

Publisher
David Dwyer

Executive Editor
Laurie Petrycki

Acquisitions Editor
Katie Purdum

Managing Editor
Sarah Kearns

Project Editor
Caroline Wise

Copy Editor
Keith Cline

Indexer
Cheryl Lenser

Technical Editor
Kurt Granroth

Proofreader
Debra Neel

Compositor
Gina Rexrode

Translator
Alexander Liemen

About the Author

Uwe Thiem is an experienced KDE programmer/developer who has developed software for driverless vehicles, as well as system close software for UNIX. Since discovering Linux in the kernel version 0.99pl9, he has written several applications for it.

He took up GUI programming when KDE was launched after finding out that it made X programming easier by several magnitudes. Recently he has worked on making KDE 64-bit clean, and he has started the IT company SysEx (`www.SysEx.com.na`) in Windhoek, Namibia.

About the Technical Reviewer

Kurt Granroth has been doing KDE development since early 1998 and is now employed by SuSE Inc. to work on KDE full time. He received his B.S. in Computer Science from Michigan Technological University in 1997, but has been a geek for much longer then that. He now lives in Phoenix, Arizona.

Contents at a Glance

Table of Contents

Preface

A friend urged me to take a look at the then still-embryonic KDE at the beginning of 1997. After having done so, my whole attitude toward X changed within one week. Even though I was an experienced UNIX and Linux programmer, I always tried to avoid X—not as a user, of course, but as a programmer. My faint-hearted attempts to become involved in X programming always stopped quite early because of the complexity of the subject matter.

With KDE (and the underlying Qt of Troll Tech), X programming became easy for the first time (if programming can ever be said to be really easy). This is why KDE has grown from an idea to the standard desktop for Linux and why it has gained wide acceptance in the UNIX world in general within the two and a half years that have passed since Matthias Ettrich's call for programmers in October 1996.

During the past 12 months, KDE also managed to change my whole perception of Linux. Prior to KDE, Linux had always been a synonym for server (from my point of view). Stable, fast, reliable, moderate when it comes to hardware: These are the properties that made Linux the ideal operating system for servers. With KDE, Linux got the chance to gain a significant share of the desktop market for the first time.

Easy and consistent use for users on the one hand and fast, simple, and efficient development of applications for the programmers on the other hand: These two factors will enable KDE and Linux to penetrate the desktop market.

This book would like to drive this process further. More often than not, the first steps in a new development environment are the most difficult ones. Heavy reference manuals are of little help in that situation. It is the "getting started" that is needed badly. Accordingly, I have concentrated on those things needed by the KDE developer-to-be to write his first application.

I was not very interested in writing a bunch of tiny "Hello World" programs to demonstrate the use of each and every class and widget in KDE. Together, we will develop a real application during the course of the book instead. That's more fun (at least for me) and closer to actual practice.

For those who have remained skeptical of X programming thus far, I hope to open the door to software development for this new desktop. The future of desktop computing has already begun. Become part of it.

Uwe Thiem
uwe@kde.org
Windhoek, Namibia
October 1999

Acknowledgments

A book like this one is never the product of one single person. Without the help of other people, the book and its translation to English would have not been possible.

I would like to thank Kurt Granroth for going through the text and sifting out technical errors that crept in during the translation process.

My special thanks go to Keith Cline, the copy editor. His hard work on the book was invaluable and made the text readable.

Katie Purdum, the acquisitions editor, made the English edition of this book possible—no easy task with regard to the translation process and an author who just can't run the "usual" word processor on his Linux computer.

Although the Trolls of Troll Tech, the creators of Qt, did not contribute directly, it goes without saying that this the book would have not been possible without their excellent Qt library.

Countless KDE developers around the globe contributed directly or indirectly. Without them, KDE would not exist and obviously neither would this book. The open and friendly atmosphere of KDE makes it easy to ask questions without hesitating. Answers then emerge fast most of the time. This atmosphere is crucial for the speed of development and it helps the author who writes about KDE.

As a former printer, I am aware that producing a book doesn't stop when the text is ready. Many people—most of them unknown—must put their work into it until, finally, a complete product hits the shelves in bookshops. My special thanks go to these people.

My little son Mathis was annoyed by being banned from hacking on my keyboard. But more important to him was that his daddy just "wasn't there" when he needed him. My daughter Sonja had to accept a "Not now!" far too often. Even worse, a "later" wouldn't follow. My wife Ulla, who has enough to worry about with just the Namibian groundwater, carried more than her share of the household and family burdens. I thank the three of you for your patience, and I promise to become a normal human being again.

—Uwe Thiem

What's On the Web Site

All the files mentioned in this book can be found on the New Riders Web site: `http://www.newriders.com/kde`.

Tell Us What You Think!

As the reader of this book, *you* are our most important critic and commentator. We value your opinion and want to know what we're doing right, what we could do better, what areas you'd like to see us publish in, and any other words of wisdom you're willing to pass our way.

As the Executive Editor for the Linux team at Macmillan Technical Publishing, I welcome your comments. You can fax, email, or write me directly to let me know what you did or didn't like about this book—as well as what we can do to make our books stronger.

Please note that I cannot help you with technical problems related to the topic of this book, and that due to the high volume of mail I receive, I might not be able to reply to every message.

When you write, please be sure to include this book's title and author, as well as your name and phone or fax number. I will carefully review your comments and share them with the author and editors who worked on the book.

Fax: 317-581-4663

Email: `newriders@mcp.com`

Mail: Laurie Petrycki
Executive Editor
Linux/Open Source
Macmillan Technical Publishing
201 West 103rd Steet
Indianapolis, IN 46290 USA

1

Why KDE?

Some may ask why we have decided to use the *K Desktop Environment* (KDE). The most important reason is because KDE isn't just another library of widgets. Because a program based on the KDE libraries "looks" quite similar to all the other KDE programs, the average user can find his way through it very quickly. In addition, KDE applications can communicate with each other very easily. They also benefit from the Window Manager's (kwm) *Session Management*[1]. It is also possible to drag and drop between KDE applications.

To compete in the marketplace, developers must offer end users something advantageous, always something new. Although some developers get trapped on the user-expectation treadmill, many others are a bit lazy. (It's not a disgrace to admit to it.) The sentence "Good programmers write good code, excellent programmers steal excellent code" has its justification. The developer who wants to write many useful and easy-to-use programs has to steal as much as possible. KDE offers the best conditions for just such stealing, and actually makes the theft legal.

KDE is based on Qt, the class library from the Norwegian company Troll Tech (`www.troll.no`). Qt contains a rich repertoire of widgets and other classes. KDE itself contains widgets and other applications that programmers can use. For example, KDE's HTML-based Help system is available for free to every single program. Menus, toolbars, and statusbars are also available, and require very little developer input. And let's not forget the File Selector, kfile; it's hard to beat.

---

[1] *Session management makes it possible for applications to save their internal state if KDE crashes or quits for some other reason. Upon the next start of KDE, the Window Manager loads the applications with the exact same state.*

And finally, although a KDE program just automatically looks good and serious, that's not the most important fact or consideration. In the end, what is most important is that the Trolls[2] eliminated one of the most annoying sources of errors in the development of a complex program, the Callback function (discussed in greater detail later).

All in all, KDE makes it possible to write software very quickly. This book identifies KDE's most significant advantages and explains how to use them.

1.1 Oh, That's C++!

Yes! ... and your point?[3] Don't let C++ scare you away. Actually, I could leave it at that, but I feel compelled to reassure any C++-phobes with these four calming words: It's not that hard. If you know C well, C++ should be a breeze (or at least not much of a problem at all). The Trolls included some very useful tutorials with their Qt library. The tutorials provide a good introduction to Qt programming. For the C programmer, these tutorials also show how programs can be successfully developed with C++.

The program that we will develop together through the course of this book demonstrates just basic techniques. There is, however, a whole wide world of object-oriented design and object-oriented programming out there; but it is beyond the scope of this book. To learn more about C++, check out *The C++ Programming Language* (Addison-Wesley), by Bjarn Stroustrup. To learn a few tricks and tips, try *More Effective* C++ (Addison-Wesley), by Scott Meyers.

KDE was not written in C++ just to ape current fashions. Instead, KDE's more than one million lines of code significantly influenced the decision to use C++. Such complex tasks are much easier to solve in C++ than in C. C++ has definitely speeded KDE's evolution, from its first release just 18 months ago to the fully usable 1.0 version now available.

1.2 Introduction

Anyone who wants to develop programs for X faces many possibilities.

It is possible, of course, to develop a program based specifically on Xlib and its extensions. That's the way "but-what-if men" go—those who can't help but continue to tinker. Others of us (and I am including myself in this

[2] *Trolls is an amusingly appropriate term that refers to those who work at Troll Tech.*

[3] *I am not a C++ fanatic. No, definitely not. If I had my choice, I would prefer a language that enforces object-oriented programming. C++ is a viable compromise; however, it builds on the solid C base, while incorporating elements of object-oriented programming.*

description) are a little bit lazy: We want to put the seat belt on and just drive the car from Point A to Point B; we don't even want to think about all the possibilities and exigencies.

Even so, we face the dilemma of an enormous number of libraries and widget collections: Tcl/Tk, XForms, Motif, to name just a few.

1.3 Conditions

By the time this book hits the shelves, all current Linux distributions in the United States should contain all components necessary for the development of a KDE program. If a component is missing in a recent distribution, alert your distributor and/or change your distribution. Those who have personally compiled their Linux system will most likely need to install additional components or change to a newer version.

1.3.1 X

KDE is a graphical user interface (GUI) and runs under X. This means that X must be installed. To use KDE, you just need the corresponding libraries for your graphic card and the corresponding X server installed.

Unfortunately, meeting this minimum requirement to use KDE does not enable you to develop KDE programs. The X header files must exist, too. It is important, therefore, to determine whether they do exist. You can check by entering this command line:

```
ls /usr/X11R6/include/X11/X.h
```

If the file X.h displays successfully, you can assume that the header files are installed.

If X.h does not display, you must use X to install the headers. How you do this depends on the Linux distribution being used. Consult your Linux User Manual for instructions.

1.3.2 Qt 1.42

The examples in this book were developed based on Qt 1.42, but were tested with Qt 1.44. Therefore, later versions (before 2.0) should function without any problems. If Qt isn't installed on your system, you can download it from the `ftp://ftp.troll.no/qt/source`. The README file included in Qt explains how to compile and/or install Qt.

1.3.3 KDE 1.1

KDE 1.1 (or a newer version before 2.0) is available on the KDE FTP server (`ftp://ftp.kde.org/pub/kde/stable`). You can find precompiled packages for many systems on the server. In my opinion, however, KDE developers should download the source and compile it themselves. That way, if any problems arise, you can take a look directly at KDE's source code. Who knows, maybe you will be the lucky person who discovers the bug in KDE that no one has found before.

1.3.4 Compiler

All examples in this book have been compiled with egcs-1.0.2. New versions of egcs should work fine, too. Your Linux distributor should have a current version of egcs. According to information from third parties, gcc-2.8.0 can also be used.

1.3.5 Automake

Automake version 1.3 has been used. You should be able to get a newer version from your Linux distributor.

1.3.6 Autoconf

Autoconf 2.12 was used to create all the configure files in this book. Again, you should be able to get packages with newer versions from your Linux distributor.

1.4 Help!

No human can memorize the whole Application Programming Interface (API) of a development environment. Thank goodness, therefore, that it is not necessary with KDE. Both KDE and the underlying class library, Qt, are delivered with excellent online Help.

1.4.1 Qt Online Help

The location of the Qt Help on your system depends on the Linux distribution being used. The correct directory is probably `/usr/local/qt/html` if you've installed Qt by yourself.

The output of the command

```
find '/' -name 'qfile.html' -print
```

should direct you to the right location. Set the KDE File Manager (kfm) to the corresponding directory and you can see a selection like that shown in Figure 1.1.

Qt Help is written in HTML, so you can easily view it with the KDE File Manager. If you want to, however, you can use other Web browsers (such as Netscape) to view the Qt online Help.

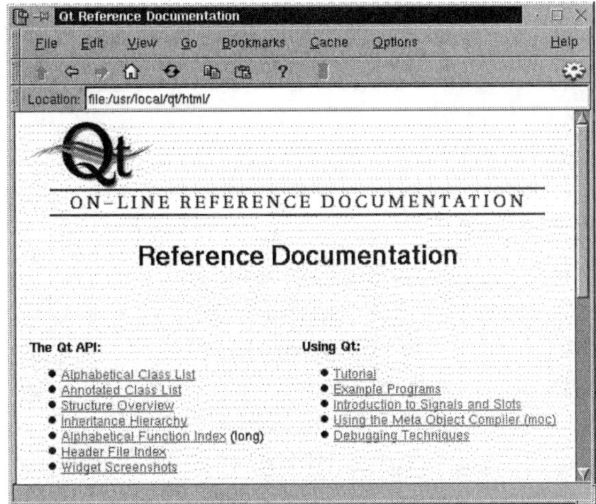

Figure 1.1 *The Qt online Help in the KDE browser.*

The Qt "newbie" should pay particular attention to "Introduction to Signals and Slots," "Tutorial," and "Examples." Anyone who works his way through the tutorials, understanding the signal-slot mechanism, is ready to write his first Qt program.[4]

A look in the "Class List" certainly won't do any harm. In particular, to get an impression about how Qt's classes are built, you should take a very close look at one of the fundamental classes (QWidget, for example). The Trolls offer some excellent Help, and you should definitely take a look here while programming.

1.4.2 KDE Online Help

KDE offers online Help as well. Sadly, KDE's Help is not distributed directly with KDE; instead, it must be created. You can create the Help by using the kdoc program from the kdesdk package[5]. You can download the kdesdk package from the KDE FTP server at `ftp://ftp.kde.org/pub/kde/`. After you have installed kdoc by doing

```
./configure
make
make install
```

in the kdesdk/kdedoc directory, you can create the KDE documentation. Assume, for example, that you want to generate the documentation in your

---

[4] *For those interested in learning more about Qt programming, I suggest* Programming with Qt, *by Kalle Dalheimer (O'Reilly).*

[5] *The kdesdk package is KDE's Software Development Kit. Although still being developed, it already contains many useful tools. The kdesdk package is discussed in more detail later in this book.*

home directory. First, you create the kdedoc directory in your home directory. Within the kdedoc directory, create a directory called kdoc-reference.

Next you must go into the directory where you can find the source of the KDE libraries, and from there to the directory kdecore. Now you enter the following command:

```
kdoc -d $HOME/kdedoc/kdecore -u file:$HOME/kdedoc/kdecore -L $HOME
kdedoc/kdoc-reference kdecore *.h
```

You can get information about the individual parameters with `kdoc -help`. This process continues for every directory in the KDE libraries. You must replace kdecore with the name of the directory for which you're creating the document. Although this might seem inconvenient (and I agree that it is), at the end when you direct your browser to $HOME/kdedoc, you'll be rewarded with a document like that shown in Figure 1.2.

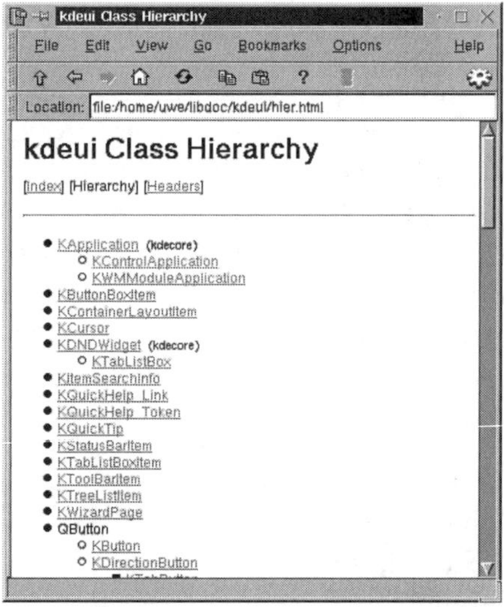

Figure 1.2 *The KDE online Help in the KDE browser.*

1.4.3 KDE Developers' Library

If you direct the KDE File Manager to `http://developer.kde.org`, you'll get to the KDE Developers' Library and with it to a selection like that shown in

Figure 1.3. This Web server is designed to satisfy the needs of the KDE developer.

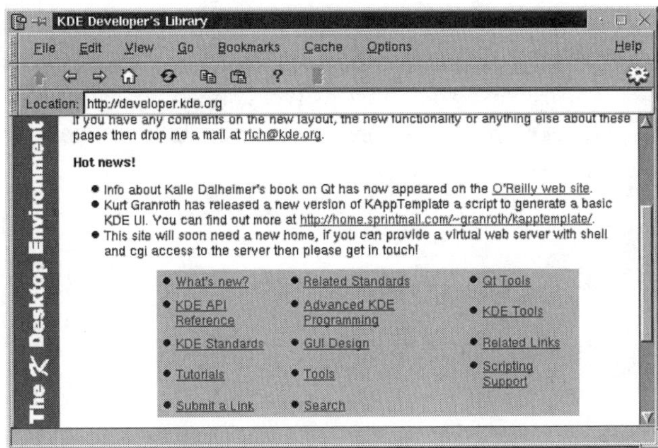

Figure 1.3 *KDE Developers' Library.*

The library contains standards that relate to the KDE API—operation of the application via the keyboard, the colour palette for icons, construction of the Help system, and so on. The library is also a rich treasure chest of tips and tricks. You can also find GUI design hints as well as descriptions of Qt and KDE tools currently available. It's worth taking a look at it from time to time, because the KDE Developers' Library is always changing and expanding. In the near future (perhaps even now as you're reading this), the library information will be available as targa files.

1.5 Which Kind of Program Am I Allowed to Write with and for KDE?

Every kind! The applications in KDE are licensed under the General Public License (GPL)[6] or other similar licenses such as the Artistic License. The libraries are under the Library General Public License (LGPL). The LGPL allows the linking of every single program to the libraries.

It's a little bit different with the underlying class of KDE, Qt. Qt is licensed under the Qt Public License. This license allows the linking of every single program, of which the source is released, against Qt without any charges. This license covers the usual freeware programs, and also covers

[6] *The exact wording of the GPL can be found on the New Riders website.*

programs that a student writes under contract with a university; these can also be linked without any charges against Qt so long as the source is released. Even the linking of commercial programs is allowed as long as the source is released.

Charges apply only if you write proprietary software, which means that you don't want to release the source. You'll need a license from the Trolls in that case.[7] Most KDE programmers will never have anything to do with the license question.

[7] *Qt, under the QPL, is a present from the Trolls to freeware developers. A special agreement between Troll Tech and the KDE organization ensures that there will always be a free Qt version (even if the Trolls go bankrupt or another company acquires them).*

2

The First KDE Program: KTsp

Okay, enough talk. Let's write something. It's time to create your first KDE program. First, create the kde directory in your home directory and copy ktsp-0.0.1.tgz into it. You can decompress the archive with

```
tar -xzvf ktsp-0.0.1.tgz
```

Change to the directory kde/ktsp-0.0.1 and enter the following sequence of commands:

```
./configure
make[1]
make install[2]
```

No errors should occur while compiling, linking, or installing; therefore, you can instantly test your handiwork. First click on K, and then click on Panel. The panel will re-initialize its menu items. Now you can find the TSP Optimizer[3] under K, Applications. Click on it. After a short time, the main window of KTsp displays onscreen, as shown in Figure 2.1.

Figure 2.1 *The KTsp's main window (version 0.0.1).*

[1] *If you are a bit short of RAM, this might take quite a long time to compile (especially as the program becomes more complex later).*

[2] *If KDE is installed system wide, and not just in your home directory, KTsp will also be installed for the whole system. To do this, you must have root rights.*

[3] *Later you will learn how to get items for all the KDE-supported languages.*

This window contains a menubar with two items on it: File and Help. It also has a toolbar with two symbols on it: The switch is an Exit Program symbol; the question mark is a Help symbol. A statusbar also appears in this window. But more is going on behind the scenes: Qt's Event Loop takes care of all events (mouse movements, mouse clicks, key presses, and so on); there is also a complete Help system (where we still have to enter text and other such things).

You can quit the program by selecting Quit from the File menu. You can also terminate KTsp from anywhere in the program by pressing Ctrl+Q—a shortcut key combination (also shown on the File menu). This particular key combination is language independent. With the File menu open, pressing Q (the underlined letter in the menu) is yet another way to terminate KTsp. Be aware, however, that the language you have installed does determine this key.

The Help menu contains three items: Contents, About KTsp, and About KDE. To get to KDE's HTML-based Help system, just click on Contents or press the F1 function key. At this time, the Help system is not so, well, helpful. We will return to it later to fix it up a bit. The other two items on the Help menu open information windows (whose content should be clear).

All these things are mostly presents from Qt and KDE! Now before losing ourselves in minutia (both large and small), let's take a quick look at how little code the "lazy" programmer has to write to create a functioning structure for an application.

```
#include <kapp.h>
#include "KTsp.h"

int main( int argc, char* argv[] )
  {
  KApplication app( argc, argv );
  KTsp* ktsp = new KTsp;
  CHECK_PTR( ktsp );
  ktsp->show();
  return app.exec();
  }
```

The entire main program consists of only five lines! We create an instance of KApplication with the name "app" and pass all parameters that KTsp has been called with.

KApplication filters such parameters that it understands by itself. Next, we create an instance of our own class KTsp, which is derived from

KTMainWindow (KTMW). KTMainWindow registers the instance automatically as the top (or main) KApplication window. Because we create the instance of ktsp on the heap, it is important to check the third line to determine whether enough memory is available. The macro CHECK_PTR will automatically exit the program (with the corresponding error message) if not enough memory is available. Line four causes the widget ktsp to show itself onscreen. At the end, we relinquish control of the program to KApplication.

The declaration of our own class KTsp still looks pretty simple:

```
class KTsp : public KTMainWindow
  {
  Q_OBJECT

  public:
    KTsp();
    ~KTsp(){};

  protected slots:
    void slotToolbarClicked( int item );
    void slotQuit();
  protected:
    void setupMenubar();
    void setupToolbar();
    void setupStatusbar();

private:
    enum { TOOLBAR_QUIT, TOOLBAR_HELP };
    enum { STATUSBAR_MESSAGE };
    QWidget *w;
  };
```

We derive KTsp from KTMainWindow. Because our program doesn't currently have any functionality of its own, we can do with just a few declarations of member functions[4]. Q_OBJECT and slots are expressions of Qt which we will discuss in greater detail in Section 2.3 "Signals and Slots."

You're probably asking yourself, "When do I use uppercase (capital letters) and lowercase (small letters)?" No need to continue pondering this weighty question: Just read on. By popular agreement (among Qt and KDE programmers), all member functions begin with a lowercase letter (except constructors and destructors). If the name of a method contains more than one word, all the following words begin with an uppercase letter. This convention makes it easier to read source code from other people (as long as everyone follows it).

---

[4] *I use the terms member function and method as synonyms for a function that is an element of a class.*

Now it's time to proceed to the constructor of KTsp:

```
KTsp::KTsp()

  {

  // create the main widget of KTsp
  w = new QWidget ( this. "Main Widget");

  // check whether the main widget could be created
  CHECK_PTR( w );

  // KTMainWindow::setView() tells KTMW that w is
  // our main widget
  setView( w );

  // set up a menubar
  setupMenubar();

  // set up a toolbar
  setupToolbar();

  // set up a statusbar
  setupStatusbar();

  }
```

First, we create an instance of QWidget, which serves as the usable area for our main window (which we don't have to do anything with at this point). We register this instance as the main widget of KTMainWindow. We call the constructor of QWidget with two parameters.

The first parameter (`this`) is a pointer to our instance `ktsp` of KTsp; thus, both `ktsp` and `w` are in a parent-child relationship (with `ktsp` as the parent). If `ktsp` is destroyed, all children are deleted simultaneously (as is `w`).[5] The second parameter, "Main Widget", is a Qt internal name for the instance. The name isn't really useful with the current Qt release. However, the Trolls promise that it will be useful for debugging in future versions. We're depending on that promise, and are therefore going ahead and giving all widgets a specific name.

The rest of the constructor consists of three calls to member functions. The calls create the menubar, the toolbar, and the statusbar. The following section takes a closer look at these calls.

2.1 Presents from KTMainWindow

KTMainWindow is one of the finest classes in KDE. It generously presents you with a menubar, a toolbar, and a statusbar; and, thanks to KDE, you don't have to concern yourself later with these features unless you want to

[5] *If a widget is declared as a child of another widget, the lazy programmer won't have to bother deleting the child. The parent widget will automatically take care of that in its own destruction.*

change them. Menubars can appear at the top or at the bottom of the window. Toolbars can be at the top, right, or left in the main window. The programmer really doesn't have to bother with such placement (unless he's exercising a specific preference). You can also de-link menubars and toolbars from the main window so that they appear independently on the desktop. Figure 2.1 shows the bars with their default placement.

KTMW is good, but not yet perfect. A substantial weakness of KTMW is that it is very difficult to calculate the exact width and height of the available space for a personalized presentation. If the programmer doesn't want a scrollbar for the main window, for example, but instead wants to align everything exactly in the available space, he must consider every possible placement of the menubar and the toolbar. Lazy programmers certainly don't want to do this. Perhaps by the time you are reading this book, this will have been made easier.

2.1.1 Menubar

Although KTWM provides a free menubar, it naturally can't know which items you want to have on the bar. Although you'll have to do this on your own, it's rather easy.

void KTsp::setupMenubar()

```
{
// Each entry in a Menubar is of the type QPopupMenu.
// So we need at least one of them.
QPopupMenu *p = new QPopupMenu;
CHECK_PTR( p );

// Create the whole file menu (for now just containing quit).
int id = p->insertItem( i18n( "&Quit" ),this, SLOT( slotQuit() ) );

// The file menu p goes into the menubar.
menuBar()->insertItem(i18n( "&File" ), p);

// KDE will generate an appropriate help menu for us. We just have to
// provide the 'About KTsp' entry.
p = kapp->getHelpMenu(false,
                      i18n( "KTsp - The TSP Optimizer\n"
                            "Version 0.0.1\n\n"
                            "(c) 1999 Uwe Thiem\n"
                            "uwe@kde.org"));
menuBar()->insertSeparator();
menuBar()->insertItem( i18n( "&Help" ), p );

}
```

Every item on the menubar consists of a QPopupMenu in which individual items are inserted. First, you create an instance of QPopupMenu. Next, you insert the `"Quit"` entry into the File menu; Quit is then instantly connected to the method `slotQuit()` so that the method gets called if the user clicks on the menu item. Because you have only one item in the File menu, you can instantly place it on the menubar.

The Help menu is next. Fortunately, KApplication creates all three necessary items: Contents, About KTsp, and About KDE. Naturally, we must provide the text for About KTsp.

The cautious reader is probably saying, "Hey, hold on a minute. We use the same pointer for both menus. Now we don't have one that points to the first menu. How should we free the memory?" Don't fret; we keep the menus over the whole runtime anyway, and most importantly, the reader isn't that lazy yet! When we placed each menu onto the menubar, we instantly gave the responsibility to the menubar. If necessary, the menubar will destroy the relevant menu and free the memory. Therefore, you can use the same pointer when creating other menus without having to worry about not being able to free the memory later.

We insert a separator before placing the Help menu onto the menubar so that we can operate KDE in two substantially different styles. Under K, Options, Desktop, Style, we can change between Windows 95 style and Motif style. The separator has no impact on the menubar in the Windows style. In Motif style, the separator ensures that the Help menu always appears on the right side of the menubar (the usual Motif "look").

Another thing needs to be cleared up: What exactly is `i18n( "string" )`? It's an abbreviation for internationalization. Because that is way too many letters for KDE developers (remember the "lazy" description earlier?), they used only the first and the last character and used `18` as a replacement for the 18 lost (unused) characters. This `i18n()` makes sure that all character strings that have to be displayed onscreen can be translated in every KDE-supported language. If this piques your interest and you want more details, you can find them in Section 2.2.1, "Internationalization," and in Chapter 8, "Localization." For the time being, make sure to use `i18n()` to enclose all strings that are supposed to be displayed.

2.1.2 Toolbar

Just as it provided a free menubar, KTMW also provides a toolbar (or as many as you want). Naturally, KTMW can't know what you actually want or need on the toolbar. So, don't start snoozing yet; we have to write some code.

---

void KTsp::setupToolbar()

```
{
// Some buttons for the toolbar. The pics are standard,
```

```
// we don't have to provide them.
toolBar()->insertButton( Icon( "exit.xpm" ),
                         TOOLBAR_QUIT, true, i18n("Exit" ) );
toolBar()->insertButton( Icon( "help.xpm" ),
                         TOOLBAR_HELP, true, i18n("Help" ) );

// and connect the whole toolbar to a slot
connect( toolBar(), SIGNAL( clicked( int ) ),
         SLOT( slotToolbarClicked(int ) ) );
}
```

That wasn't so difficult, was it? And, it is certainly not much code for a toolbar that the user can place inside and outside the main window (even while the program is running). You enter every button with a single line of code in the order that the buttons should be placed from left to right on the toolbar:

```
toolbar()->insertButton( Icon( "icon.xpm" ), int id,
                         bool enabled,i18n( "toolTipText" ) )
```

You pass `Icon()` the name of a little graphic. It finds the graphic on every system, loads it, and returns a QPixmap reference. As long as KDE is installed correctly on your system, it doesn't matter in which of the many possible directories the graphic file is really situated.[6] It will be found. As the next parameter `int id`, you pass a unique value with which you can later identify the single buttons. With `bool enabled`, you decide whether the buttons are enabled or disabled at the beginning: True means enabled, false disabled. Later, you will also be able to directly switch a single button on or off during runtime. Finally, with `"toolTipText"`, you set the text that displays in the little rectangle that appears under the button when the mouse cursor stays over it for a short time. Obviously, you internationalize the text with `i18n()`.

You must repeat this line of code for every button that you want to display on the toolbar. Finally, with `connect()`, you make sure that your method `slotToolbarClicked()` is called when the user clicks on one of the toolbar entries. With this, you have successfully constructed your toolbar.

Perhaps you have noticed some KDE programs that don't just have buttons with little graphics on the toolbar, but have other elements as well (KLyX and KFinger, for example). Actually, KTMW knows more methods to insert elements into the toolbar than just `toolBar()->insertButton()`. In addition, several widgets are also usable. Special insert methods adapt the widgets on the toolbar for combo boxes, frames and editable lines. The programmer still has to adjust other widgets on his own.

---

[6] *In fact,* `Icon()` *searches in several system-wide directories, depending on your system's configuration; after that, it searches in the hidden directory, .kde, in your home directory. You can find more details about it at* `kiconloader.h` *in* `kdelibs/kdecore`.

2.1.3 Statusbar

I can't say much about the statusbar for now. We just use it to display text.

void KTsp::setupStatusbar()

```
{
// A very simple statusbar for now.
statusbar()->insertItem( i18n( "ready" ), STATUSBAR_READY );
}
```

This is all self explanatory. Later we'll do more interesting things with the statusbar. We'll divide it into different fields and display dynamic texts. For now, however, we can be content with the free statusbar, in which we can easily display text.

2.2 Presents from KApplication

The presents from KApplication aren't as visible as the ones from KTMW. We've seen some in the source code of our program, KTsp. Some are discussed here. Others are discussed later as their importance becomes relevant.

The following sections run through the various KApplication present.

2.2.1 Internationalization

Every program that wants international acknowledgement can't just restrict itself by supporting only one language. Further, it can't restrict itself by supporting only a given set of languages.

The ideal case is reached when all other languages can be added later without changing anything in the executable program. The ambitious user should be able to add his own native language to the already integrated ones if it isn't already supported.

KDE developers understood this ideal early so that they were able to effect it in KDE. At the time of this writing, KDE supports over 30 languages. Some are not yet completed, but the translators are at work on them. By the time you are actually reading this book, KDE might support even more languages.

You have already seen the expression `i18n( "Some text" )` multiple times. It's actually a macro in kapp.h, and expands to `KApplication::getApplication->getLocale()->translate( "Some text" )`. This should make it clear why this macro is defined. The function `translate()` is an element function of the class `KLocale` (`klocale.h`), which is declared as follows:

```
const char *translate( const char *index )
```

We pass a pointer to a string to `translate()` and get a pointer to a string back. One KDE database contains translations of common expressions such as `"Open"`, `"File"`, and `"Options"`. Another KDE database has every program that contains translations of expressions used specifically by this program.

`translate()` first searches in the program-specific database. If it can't find anything, it then searches in the KDE-wide database. This provides us with a standard set of common translations that we don't have to worry about in our program. Be aware, however, that it also makes it possible to overwrite KDE-wide translations (if our translation doesn't fit within the context of a specific program, for example).

If no translation is found in either database, `translate()` returns the string which was given as the parameter earlier. This makes it possible to work with unfinished translations, too.

The passed pointer is used as the index while searching the databases. Although this method is very flexible and doesn't require any special identification for expressions, it still sounds rather slow. Don't be fooled, however; `translate()` is actually implemented so that there won't be any distinct delay on today's computers.

KDE is still based on the ASCII character set. That's why the possibilities of supporting languages are limited to languages that can be expressed with ASCII. Qt 2.0, which is probably available with the release of this book, will support Unicode. Unicode is a 16-bit character set that provides enough characters for all the "living" languages. With it, KDE has the possibility to speak all languages (at least that's the goal).

You're not just reading this book for fun, are you? My guess is that you probably plan on developing KDE software. Even if you don't see any reason why your program should support multiple languages, you should at least internationalize it with `i18n()`. This isn't much work, and doing so makes it possible for other users to integrate their language into the program without changing the source code. Who knows, maybe you will change your mind in a year. Then you'll certainly be glad about your decision to include the possibility.

2.2.2 Help

KApplication gives us two presents that we can use while creating a Help system for the user. You have already learned about one:

```
p = kapp->getHelpMenu( false,
                       i18n( "KTsp - The TSP Optimizer\n"
                             "Version 0.0.1\n\n"
                             "(c) 1999 Uwe Thiem\n"
                             "uwe@kde.org" ) );
```

This little code provides a complete Help menu. The only thing that you have to contribute to this is the information about the program itself and the author.

The other present is hidden in a piece of code that hasn't appeared in this book up to now:

void KTsp::slotToolbarClicked(int item)

```
{
// Handle all buttons in toolbar.
switch (item)
  {
  case TOOLBAR_QUIT:
    slotQuit();
    break;
  case TOOLBAR_HELP:
    kapp->invokeHTMLHelp( "", "" );
    break;

  default:
    // OOps! This shouldn't happen.
    break;
  }
}
```

This element function will be called if the user clicks on a button on the toolbar. The identification of the clicked item is passed to the method as a parameter. `slotToolbarClicked()` uses this parameter to decide which button is meant. It is possible to give every button its own element function, too. For now, however, the interesting instruction is `kapp->invokeHTMLHelp( "", "" )`.

With a single line of source code we call a complete Help system, which doesn't just find out where our documentation is saved, but also instantly starts the HTML browser that displays it. Two parameters are passed to `invokeHTMLHelp()`; both are strings. The first is the logical name of the program, which is necessary if it differs from the actual one. If we pass an empty string, the actual name of the program is used to find the documentation. The second string is more useful. It allows context-sensitive Help. At some location in our program, we could use `kapp->invokeHTMLHelp( "", i18n( "Menubar" ) )`. This would take us directly to the location in our documentation.

Apart from that which we quite obviously have to write for our documentation, this is all that we need in the source code of our program. The lazy programmer is happy, and can invest his time in the functionality of the program.

2.2.3 More Presents

As you can tell from the preceding discussion, KDE is not about hours, days, months, or years writing code. Instead, the focus is on the structure, Session Management, and savable configuration of the application. So far, we've yet to discuss Session Management or savable configuration issues. That's about to change.

Under Session Management, the internal state of the program (loaded, edited, or created files) as well as the exterior state of the program (where and on which desktop the program's window(s) has been opened) are saved at the termination of KDE. When KDE is started the next time (next `"Session"`), the Window Manager will restore the correct state of the program at the correct desktop and at the exact location.

This means that a text editor will be loaded with the correct file (maybe even with changes that hadn't been saved yet) on the desktop at the next session. Try it with the KDE editor KWrite.

It really works! Clearly, the application programmer must save the inner state of the program correctly by himself. How exact this state is saved is left to the programmer. KWrite remembers where the cursor was, for example. Chapter 7, "Session Management," discusses this in more detail.

The other present is savable configuration. It means that we can make our program configurable and save the configuration at the termination of the program. Everything can be saved from the size of the window to very program-specific things such as the preferred drawing tool (pen, brush, spray can) in a drawing program. The corresponding settings load at the next start of the program.

After the programmer arranges to save the settings, he doesn't have to monitor that save; KDE *will* save the configuration settings. By the time our KTsp has properties that are worth saving, we will discuss this in more detail (see Section 5.2, "KConfig").

2.3 Signals and Slots

Finally, we're at one of the most interesting features that Qt provides. This time KDE has nothing to do with it. The concept of signals and slots is completely realized in Qt. KDE just uses it.

What happens if the user presses the *N* key or clicks the left mouse button, but X sends an event notice that says something like "*N* pressed" or "Left mouse button pressed at position 228, 175." With this information, the application programmer could hunt down the widget where the mouse was pressed. This would be an unbelievably boring task and could produce tons of errors in the source code, not to mention all the time that it would take. "Who would want to do all this?" you ask. Well, that's a fair question. All that hunting is not the task of the application. It's the job of the underlying toolkit. The underlying toolkit finds out in which widget the mouse has been used, whether it was pressed, and whether it was clicked or double-clicked. In reality, all toolkits that live up to the name "toolkit" perform this function. Qt certainly does.

The next problem is, what do we do with this? The user has clicked on the Quit button. The application programmer has written the code, somewhere, which is supposed to be executed. How?

2.3.1 The Disadvantages of Previous Solutions

The solution to this problem is controversial. Many toolkits use the so-called Callback function. The application registers its own code, which is supposed to be executed at the widget (the Quit button in this example). You can do this by giving a function pointer to the widget.

If the user clicks on the Quit button, the code will be executed over the corresponding pointer to the function. This is, so to speak, pure C! So far so good.

For the registration, the widget expects a pointer to function with a set number of parameters and a specific return type. Unfortunately, the compiler can't check this, which means that there's no real "type" safety. The programmer must register the "right" function at the widget. Every time we hear, "The programmer has to...," it definitely means more work for the programmer. In this case, it also means less security. If the programmer registers a function with different numbers of parameters or with parameters of the false type or with a false return type, the application will most likely crash. This is annoying both for the user and for the programmer (who must then put more work into his program to find this bug). If the project is big and complex enough, a lot of faults are inevitable. Callback functions can become a nightmare.[7]

Some toolkits take another approach, corresponding with the C++ philosophy. Widgets already contain element functions such as `pressed()`, `released()`, and `clicked()`. They're declared virtually and the implementation doesn't do anything on its own. The programmer derives his own widgets from the ones provided by the toolkit and overwrites the methods that are of interest to him.

---

[7] *Be aware also of the beloved, but still unfounded, assumptions (like an* `int` *being the same as a* `void`*. Assumptions don't count on 64-bit DEC Alpha systems; instead, they just make more faults possible.*

With a Quit button, we probably don't have be concerned about `pressed()` and `released()`—at least I can't think of any logical use (so it's okay with us that they don't do anything). We'll only overwrite `clicked()` and insert the code for our own version of the function that will be called at the termination of the program. It'll probably check whether the program contains changed data and a corresponding dialog box that asks whether the data should be saved.

This sounds a lot better. We won't jump around in the program over pointers to functions, but a class does what it was made for. Although the compiler guarantees type safety, something still seems amiss. Imagine a program with hundreds rather than just a few dialog boxes, buttons, icons, and combo boxes. The poor programmer will have to derive classes the whole time even though he wants to check only one button. This won't be a problem so long as we provide a small user interface with some menus, a few dialog boxes, and some icons on the toolbar. If, on the other hand, we provide an rich interface, we must write hundreds of lines of code—when what we really want to do is concentrate on the functionality of our program.

Other ways exist to fix this problem. In the Windows world, it's normal to use macros, for example; but they can never provide any type safety. All the previously discussed ways are absolutely practical and not just theoretical, but all have at least one disadvantage. They definitely mean more work for the developer because they're either insecure and lead to a lot of debugging, or they demand so many lines of code from the beginning. That's something for workaholics. We want it easier!

2.3.2 A New Approach: Signals and Slots

We want type safety and as little code as possible. The Trolls responded to our demands with a new way, their own signals and slots. To say it right at the beginning: The signals in Qt represent something totally different from UNIX signals, although both of them are a kind of asynchronous communication.

The idea behind this is that a widget sends a signal to inform its environment that something has changed in the widget. In our example, the Quit button sends the signal `clicked()`. For the widget, it doesn't matter whether something will receive the signal. It informed its surroundings (the program as the whole), "I've been clicked," and the widget has fulfilled its responsibility. Actually, this orientates the C++ way more than the virtual methods discussed in the preceding section. It's really not the responsibility of the Quit button to check whether the data of the program has been changed and whether to start other actions.

The code that should be executed at the termination of the program now has to know that the signal is sent; otherwise, this whole exercise would be pretty senseless. Slots are the receivers. They're actually normal member functions distinguished so that Qt can connect signals to them. The implementation of a slot is the code executed when the signal is received. Before going into detail, take a look at this little example:

```
class MyClass : QWidget
{
Q_OBJECT
public:
  MyApp();
  virtual ~MyApp();

signals:
  void colourChanged( int colour );

public slots:
  void changeColour( int colour );

private:
  int _colour;
};
```

First, take a look at `Q_OBJECT`. Every class declaration that contains signals or slots has to have `Q_OBJECT`, too (discussed in more detail later). As you can see, the new keywords signals and slots are used like normal access specifiers. We declared the signal `colourChanged( int colour; )`, which obviously should be sent when the widget changes its colour.

The programmer never implements a signal; he can declare it only. Qt takes care of the implementation by itself. The return type is always `void`. A signal can have an unlimited number of parameters of any type. You should, however, use standard types such as `int`, `char`, and `float`, and avoid using self-defined types. That's how to make sure that slots that have nothing to do with self-defined types can be connected with the signals; it just makes the whole mechanism more flexible.

The return type of a slot is just like the one of the signal, always `void`. Just like signals, slots can have an unlimited number of parameters of any type. Standard types should be used here as well, just like with the signals. Unlike with signals, we will assign access specifiers to the slots. Their meanings are obvious:

- *Public Slots*—Every class can connect signals with it.
- *Protected Slots*—Only the class itself and the derived classes can connect signals with it.
- *Private Slots*—Only the class itself can connect signals to it.

Besides this, every slot can be declared as virtual. Most of the slots that you'll encounter will be public slots. A slot is actually no more than a member function that can connect to signals. That's why the programmer must implement it, because this is the place where the answer to the signal has to be defined. No one except the programmer can know this. The implementation of the slot `changeColour()` in the example class MyClass, above, could be as follows:

MyClass::changeColour(int colour)

```
{
if ( _colour != colour )
  {
  _colour = colour;
  // Do whatever is necessary to actually change the colour
  emit colourChanged( _colour );
  }
}
```

MyClass receives the signal telling it to change the colour. After that, MyClass decides whether the colour actually will have to be changed. If that's the case, it will memorize the new colour, change the colour corresponding to the received signal, and inform its surroundings that the change of the colour has taken place by sending the signal `colourChanged()`. If the signal should be sent within the first IF block or after it (this means regardless of whether the colour has really changed) depends on what the surroundings will do with it.

Another keyword, besides signal and slot, that you need to be familiar with is emit. As its name implies, emit sends a signal without the programmer having to worry about who receives it.

But how does the signal reach the right slot? `QObject::connect ( QObject *sender, const char *signal, QObject *receiver, const char *member)` is responsible for this where sender is the object that sends the signal; signal the name of the signal, receiver the Object that receives that signal, and member the name of the slot. Qt defines two macros that make the whole thing easier. Assume, for example, that we have a second class like the following:

class Test : QObject

```
  {
  Q_OBJECT

  public:
    Test();
    virtual ~Test();
```

continues ▶

class Test : QObject continued

```
signals:
  void forceColourChange( int colour );

public slots:
  void slaveHasColourChanged( int colour );
};
```

An instance of this class should be able to force the class MyClass to change the colour and report a successful change. To create the corresponding connection between signals and slots, we need the following piece of code:

```
MyClass myclass;
Test test;

  connect( &myclass, SIGNAL( colourChanged( int ) ),
           &test, SLOT( slaveHasColourChanged( int ) ) );
  connect( &test, SIGNAL( forceColourChange( int ) ),
           &myclass, SLOT( changeColour( int ) ) );
```

This variant of `connect()` needs all four parameters and can be used at anytime and anywhere. To save us some work, a whole set of function variants exist. If the connection takes place within an element function of the class to which the signal also belongs, for example, you can disregard the first parameter (which is similar to the third parameter). It's even possible to just pass the signal and the slot. In such a case, `connect()` will be in the class to which both the signal and the slot belong.

Take a look at a line in `KTsp::setupMenubar()`, for example:

```
int id = p->insertItem( i18n( "&Quit" ),this, SLOT( slotQuit() ) );
```

We don't just insert the Quit button in the File menu with this line, we also simultaneously specify the slot that should be connected to the signal `clicked()` of the menu entry Quit. The method `insertItem()`executes `connect()` for us. The discussion thus far has focused on widgets in the connection with signals and slots, but actually that isn't quite right.

Everything we need for this is already implemented in `QObject`. Therefore, we can let classes, which don't display themselves onscreen, also communicate over signals and slots. This gets interesting when we have a class with an extensive calculating task in the background and which is supposed to report itself when it finishes. We can just derive it from `QObject` and send the signal `done()` when its work is finished. This is discussed later, and you will really get a chance to use it.

Assume that you have created a new instance of a class with `new`, for example, and then connected its signals and slots with other signals and slots. If you were to destroy this instance with `delete`, what would happen? Qt, without complaint and oh-so friendly, would clean it up. You don't need to destroy the connections between the corresponding signals and slots (although you may). In programs that permanently create and destroy connections during runtime, you must perform this work by yourself. There's a function that you can use, as follows:

```
QObject::disconnect( QObject *sender, const char *sender,
                     QObject *receiver,
 const char *member )
```

It has the same syntax as `connect()`. In this example, you would destroy the connections with the following two lines:

```
disconnect( &myclass, SIGNAL( colourChanged( int ) ),
            &test, SLOT( slaveHasColourChanged( int ) ) );
disconnect( &test, SIGNAL( forceColourChange( int ) ),
            &myclass, SLOT( changeColour( int ) ) );
```

Actually, the example program doesn't use `disconnect()` even one time. In rare cases, however, this function proves useful.

2.3.3 The Meta Object Compiler (moc) and How It Is Used

The preceding section explained that only the programmer declares signals; Qt implements them. Naturally Qt can't intervene in the compiler itself (except through the pre-processor). So how does Qt implement signals?

The Trolls have developed another useful tool: the Meta Object Compiler (moc). It generates C++ source code from the class declarations that contain signals and slots, which you can compile and link to the program.

There's not much to say about moc. It's used like this:

```
moc -o mysource.moc.cpp mysource.h
```

The syntax is as expected from a compiler. Some people call moc another pre-processor and because pre-processors are rightfully taboo (except `#include`), most people reject moc. Moc is actually a Meta Object Compiler and not a pre-processor. A pre-processor actually changes parts of the source code so that the compiler gets something different as input from what is in the source; moc, on the other hand, generates additional source code from the header files.

You may be asking yourself, "How can the compiler compile something that uses the new keywords signal, slot, and emit?" The compiler doesn't know them! In this case, the pre-processor is really used. It eliminates these keywords before the compiler gets to see the source.

2.4 Accelerator Keys and Shortcuts

Among user types, you're bound to come across the "mouse clicker" as well as the "keyboard hacker." Everyone who writes a lot with his computer gets annoyed with programs that force you to take your hands from the keyboard and use the mouse to perform a specific task. That's why every programmer should ensure that his program can be used as much as possible with the keyboard, too. Okay, there are exceptions: Freehand drawing in a graphics program is hard to effect with the keyboard. On the other hand, a dialog box on an editor window that has syntax highlighted, but is only accessible with the mouse, is aggravating.

Perhaps you've wondered about the ampersand (&) in each menu item at the introduction of the menu bar.

Consider this line, for example:

```
int id = p->insertItem( i18n( "&Quit" ),this, SLOT( slotQuit() ) );
```

If an ampersand appears in front of a letter, an underline "highlights" that letter. All menus can be activated with the Alt key and the underline key. The Alt key is used, for example, because the user could be in an editor. The editor program would not be able to differ between an *f* that is written in the text and an *f* that should open the File menu. When the menu is activated, the modifier isn't used anymore because it is then clear that the menu items are of interest. If you open the File menu in the program KTsp with Alt+F, you can see that the *Q* of Quit is underlined. Pressing *Q* (when the menu is activated) terminates the program.

This mechanism is already provided by Qt. The Trolls call it *accelerator keys*. We're dealing with a method to go through a menu system step by step and then execute the desired action. The programmer must ensure that the same key isn't used multiple times as an accelerator within a menu.

The two items "Save" and "Save as" must be written as "&Save" and "Save &as" in the source code. By the way, it doesn't matter whether capitals or small letters are highlighted.

It's immediately clear that the accelerator keys are language dependent. At the translation of menus, you should pay attention to logically place the ampersand in front of letters.

KDE provides another method to control programs from the keyboard: shortcuts. This method differs completely from the accelerator keys and doesn't just work with menus. A key plus a modifier (such as the Ctrl key) is directly bound to an action. Execute the program KTsp and press Ctrl+Q. KTsp will terminate.

The class KAccel provides shortcut functionality. (Shortcuts are different from accelerator keys. Shortcut functionality is provided by class KAccel.

What? KAccel? I guess we can thank KDE developers for the confusing name!) It's now time to confess that I cheated a bit while introducing the source code for the menu system. To avoid making things needlessly complicated, I left everything out that had anything to do with shortcuts. Take a gander at how `KTsp::setupMenubar()` really looks:

void KTsp::setupMenubar()

```
  {
  // Create an KAccel instance
  accel = new KAccel( this );

  // Each entry in a Menubar is of the type QPopupMenu.
  //So we need
  //at least one of them.
  QPopupMenu *p = new QPopupMenu;
  CHECK_PTR( p );

  // Create a file menu, connect the accelerator key to our slot,
  //and tell KAccel to show the key in the menu.
  int id = p->insertItem( i18n( "&Quit" ), this,
                          SLOT( slotQuit()
) );

  accel->connectItem( KAccel::Quit, this, SLOT( slotQuit() ) );
  accel->changeMenuAccel( p, id, KAccel::Quit );

  // The file menu p goes into the Menubar.
  menuBar()->insertItem( i18n( "&File" ), p );

  // KDE will generate an appropriate help menu for us.
  //We just have to provide the 'About KTsp' entry.
  p = kapp->getHelpMenu( false,
                         i18n( "KTsp - The TSP Optimizer\n"
                               "Version 0.0.1\n\n"
                               "(c) 1999 Uwe Thiem\n"
                               "uwe@kde.org" ) );

  menuBar()->insertSeparator();
  menuBar()->insertItem(i18n( "&Help" ), p );

}
```

First, we create an instance of the class KAccel. After we've created the menu item Quit, we connect the predefined shortcut `KAccel::Quit` with the slot `slotQuit()`, as follows:

```
accel->connectItem( KAccel::Quit, this, SLOT( slotQuit() ) );
```

`KAccel::Quit` is defined as Ctrl+Q. The next line is:

```
accel->changeMenuAccel( p, id, KAccel::Quit );
```

By modifying the menu item and showing the shortcut, the user will eventually learn the shortcut; `p` is the `QpopupMenu`, and `id` allows `changeMenuAccel()` to change the right item.

`KAccel::Quit` is the predefined shortcut again. KDE knows a total of 18 of these shortcuts, as identified in the following table.

Action	Shortcut
Close	Ctrl+W
Copy	Ctrl+C
Cut	Ctrl+X
End	Ctrl+End
Help	F1
Home	Ctrl+Home
Insert	Ctrl+Insert
New	Ctrl+N
Next	PageDown
Open	Ctrl+O
Paste	Ctrl+V
Print	Ctrl+P
Prior	PageUp
Quit	Ctrl+Q
Replace	Ctrl+R
Save	Ctrl+S
Undo	Ctrl+Z

Not all these shortcuts are useful in every program. The programmer has to decide which ones he wants to use. Then the developer defines the exact meaning in the context of the program by connecting the corresponding slots with the shortcuts. In an editor, Next is certainly the next page; in a graphics program, however, it probably refers to the next picture. After all is said and done, the lazy programmer can essentially rely on a set of predefined shortcuts that cover most actions.

Shortcuts are language independent! No matter which language the KDE user activates, Ctrl+Q is always Quit. Although in some languages the shortcut designations might look a bit strange, the language-independent consistency does make the shortcuts easier to remember and, therefore, easier to use.

3

KTsp is Supposed to Do Something

So far, we have created a program that can display a window on the desktop and can be terminated. Other than that, it can't do anything else. For an application with a graphical interface, that's really no mean feat. Our program should *do* something, and we should be able to do something with the program—use dialog boxes, load and save files, and so forth.

I'm sure that you've had your fill of "Hello World" programs, and I'm really not in the mood to write another (Are you?). They don't really do anything. Instead, I have decided to advance one program through the course of this book until we have a real application at the end. Our first steps were pretty simple, but now it's time to get some functionality into the program.

3.1 The Problem: TSP

Most likely, every computer science major has been confronted with the Traveling Salesman Problem (TSP)—and has probably tortured him/herself with it. For those who might have missed the TSP experience, it's your lucky day. We're going to go through it here. After a quick introduction to the problem, I'll show you how we can use the computer to "solve" it.

On a sales trip, a traveling salesman must travel through five cities, A–E. He starts in City A and is supposed to return to City A at the end. Our salesman is practical; he wants to know the full path with the shortest distance. Because we do not have an algorithm that directly calculates the shortest path, we must calculate all of them. The question remains: how many circuits are there? They can be thought of as permutations as follows:

A-B-C-D-E

A-B-C-E-D

A-B-E-C-D

These three routes are only some of possibilities. You can imagine the ends as being connected to each other so that you have a complete circuit. If there are *n* cities, there will be n!—that is, n * (n – 1) * ... * 1—circuits. Actually, there are fewer possibilities for our salesman, because some of the routes are the same. A-B-C-D-E is the same for him as C-D-E-A-B; they both equal the same distance. Therefore, instead of n!, we have only (n – 1)! possible circuits. This number can be reduced again because A-B-C-D-E and E-D-C-B-A are the same. At the end, we're left with only (n – 1)!/2 possible circuits. With five cities, this doesn't compute to a very large number—12, in fact. With those 12, we can quite easily calculate the relative distances and quickly determine the shortest full circuit. As the number of stops (cities, in this case) increases, however, we begin to face a much more complex task.

Because calculators can display up to two-digit exponents only, they "give up" at 100 digits and display an error message. At just 70!, we reach a 100-digit number. Are you beginning to understand our little problem?

Let's assume that we want to calculate the solution of a TSP with 300 cities. Why should anybody do this? Because knowledge is power: He who knows the shortest way can finish in the quickest time. When thousands of "work pieces" (be they cities in a sales circuit, stitches in a suit, a certain number of drill holes, or whatever) must be accomplished, this knowledge provides a significant advantage. Using today's fastest computers (well, at least in this example), we can solve our 300-city TSP in a reasonable time (about half an hour).

As the number of work pieces increases, however, so does the time it takes to solve a TSP. With just 301 cities (a number we actually will deal with later), today's fastest computers need 300 times as much time to calculate (about 150 hours). This isn't reasonable at all. And the numbers don't just stop there. Assume, for example, that the fastest computer in the world can solve a TSP for 1,000 cities in half an hour. If we need the solution for 1,001 cities, we're going to have to wait for future computer generations that have approximately 1,000 times faster processing speed before we can solve this task in a reasonable amount of time. How impractical is that?

If the time needed to solve a problem increases that fast with the size of the problem, we can consider the problem unsolvable.[1] Unfortunately, many problems fit this classification.

[1] *The key term here is NP-complete problems. NP stands for "non-polynomial," and means that no polynome describes the dependence of the time the solution takes to the size of the problem. Every computer science handbook should have a section about it.*

3.2 The Solution: GDA

Let's be honest: Programmers are a breed apart. They use their skill (and perhaps a bit of magic) to get machines to do things that others can't—from the Global Positioning System (GPS) to the special effects (all based on programmed calculations) in the movie *Titanic*. That's why we (programmers) can't get over the fact that we sometimes fail in boring, everyday life. Yes, in fact, we probably really are geeks.

Many techniques have been developed to calculate better solutions for a variety of tasks. Those techniques, although beyond the scope of this book, are available in most every computer science handbook. We're not here to do math. We're here to solve a real problem.

The mathematician searches for the global optimum. The workshop manager who wants to produce his work units as cheaply as possible is pleased with a local optimum coming close to the global one. Actually, he doesn't even care about how close he comes to the global optimum so long as he gets a solution that is significantly better than the one he has used so far. If he needs 9 minutes for his work piece rather than the 10 minutes needed before, he'll be very pleased. Apart from the setup time of the drilling machine, he saves 10% of machine usage. This can add up to a lot of money.

Just like the workshop manager in the preceding paragraph, we do not have to seek the global optimum. We can give up the goal of finding the *shortest* circuit and content ourselves instead with a short circuit. That is, rather than search for the best solution, we can accept a good solution (even our definition of "good" can be flexible). We want to solve a practical task; it's not our goal to write a theoretical dissertation.

In 1990, Professor Gunter Dueck and Tobias Scheuer introduced their new Threshold Accepting Algorithm (TAA) in the *Journal of Computational Physics* in the article titled "Threshold Accepting: A General Purpose Optimization Algorithm Appearing Superior to Simulated Annealing." The exciting thing with this new algorithm was that it was fully deterministic, contrary to Simulated Annealing (SA), for example, which made extensive use of random numbers. TAA used significantly less CPU time than SA and provided at least as good results as SA.

In 1999, Professor Dueck released the article "New Optimization Heuristics—The Great Deluge Algorithm and the Record-to-Record Travel," again in the *Journal of Computational Physics*. I want to explain the Great Deluge Algorithm (GDA) a little bit. Just like the TAA, it's fully deterministic.

First we need to think of our problem scenario in three-dimensional terms, as a place. Then we can determine the lay of the land—that is, learn about the topography of the place. All the possible circuits are mapped on the XY plane; the similar ones are close to each other. In the Z direction, we determine the quality of every circuit. Because the TSP contains only discrete solutions, we won't get a continuum. Instead, we get discrete points in the solution space. We can connect these points with each other so that the whole thing looks like a grid (just like function plotters draw).

The highest peak (or summit) in the solution space obviously represents the global optimum. A lot of other peaks appear as well; these represent local optimums. The bad solutions appear, obviously, as the flat or deep areas. A priori we can't assume is this landscape's appearance: We can't know whether it will look like a dune landscape with mostly similar peak levels or more like the Himalayas with a large number of peaks with many different heights (including many high ones).

Now it's time to put GDA on a randomly chosen place in the solution space. Randomness applies in this instance only; we don't use it again. From now on, everything will be strictly deterministic. The next step is to let it rain on the landscape. With time, the water will accumulate in the valleys, and the water level will ascend until only the highest summit is left. GDA is allowed to move with little steps—this means only to flanking solutions—through the solution space. There's only one restriction: Our algorithm must not get wet feet. It can move only on dry land. The process is finished when our algorithm can't move anymore, which means that it's surrounded by water.

Our algorithm might be stranded on the summit or on a totally unimportant local optimum. However, the probability is against it. We *imagined* the solution space as three dimensional. In reality, it has a lot more dimensions mapped on the XY plane. The more dimensions, the more ways from one point to the other (and fewer impasses). Our algorithm has a lot of possibilities to move. The ascending water level cuts its way a lot less than in our three-dimensional imaginings.

Still, GDA might find itself stranded on the summit of the Spitzkoppe in Namibia,[2] but report that it is on Mount Everest. That's why we'll run GDA many times, every time from a different random place in the solution space, and use the best result. We could still get results we don't like, possibly over and over. But we can apply the practical approach (like our workshop-manager example earlier): If the result is worse than the solution we are currently using so far, we just ignore it or calculate some more until we're pleased with one. In serious applications, we would run GDA between 50

[2] *The Spitzkoppe is a mountain in the Namib Desert. Although it would be strange to see the mountain surrounded by water, we can still imagine such an event.*

and 100 times, and then use the best result. With the speed at which the algorithm performs, this is not a problem.

At the beginning when the water level is at its lowest, GDA can move relatively freely within the solution space. As the water ascends over time, however, GDA will be forced to move up the hills and finally onto a peak. The critical phase is the middle one, when GDA starts to move up a mountain range. If the water level is high enough, GDA won't get down again. Here's where it's important not to get fooled by our three-dimensional imagination. In high-dimensional spaces, there are many ways to get from one point to the other (in this case, from mountain to mountain, or even from peak to peak). The chances are extremely rare that GDA will find itself on a low mountain in the middle phase and only find ways through the water to the other mountain(s). The probability states that it's more likely that there are "dry ways." Only at the end, when only the highest peaks are above water, will GDA's movement be seriously restricted. At that point, the motto becomes: Go For It!

The rest of this book could focus on creating simulated solution spaces that can fool any conceivable optimizing algorithm, but that's not necessary; the literature is full of them. This is not a book about optimization algorithms or malicious spaces posing exceptionally big challenges for optimization algorithms. This book sticks to the assumption that problems coming from practical applications normally have good-natured solution spaces. By the way, we can test the quality of GDA by ourselves when KTsp finally does something.

We can sketch a cycle of GDA in pseudo code:

```
choose a random initial solution currentSolution;
initialize the rain speed rainSpeed > 0;
set the initial waterLevel < quality( currentSolution );
do
  {
  create a newSolution as a small change of currentSolution;
  calculate q = quality( newSolution );


  if ( q > waterLevel )
    {
    currentSolution = newSolution;
    waterLevel += rainSpeed;
    }
  } while ( accepted changes occur );
```

What is a "small change?" It depends on the concrete problem. In our case, we cut the circuit in two places and connect the loose ends to each other, crossed over. Let's use our earlier example again: A-B-C-D-E, wherein E connects with A to create a real circuit. Now we cut it at the two places between B and C on the one site and A and E on the other. Next we connect A with C and E with B. The resulting circuit is as follows:

A-B-E-D-C, wherein C closes the circle to A.

As you can instantly see, we either destroyed a crossing in the circuit with this action or we created one. Our TSP is definitely suboptimal as long as there're crossings, because there's always a shorter total way. In comparison, a crossing-free course isn't optimal, per se. There're always many crossing-free ways with every given distribution of a larger number of cities on the plane. In any case, a crossing-free way isn't bad. We can leave it to GDA to find a solution that pleases our workshop-manager practicality. The criterion for GDA is not crossing freeness, but quality, which means a "short way" in our case.

The abort condition for our loop in the pseudo code still needs an explanation. If there hasn't been any change accepted for a long time, GDA will be surrounded by water and won't be able to move anymore. In other words, GDA is on a peak (which doesn't necessarily represent the global optimum). But how long is "long?"

It depends on the concrete problem. We definitely can't use a large number of actions that all haven't been accepted. Say, for example, that if 100,000 actions haven't been accepted on one piece, we'll abort. This number would be absurdly high for a little TSP with 50 cities, and we would perform the same actions over and over again. Our program would run unnecessarily long. However, this number might be too small for a big TSP. There could be actions left that haven't yet been tested. This means that GDA could still move.

At least for TSPs, it's easy to choose the right number of actions: If the GDA has traveled through all the cities one time and tried all possibilities by cutting and connecting the circuit without finding one acceptable solution, it will abort. Every other cycle would lead only to the same actions that have already been rejected.[3] GDA can confidently assume that it's on a peak.

3.3 Totally Abstract GDA Implementation

We want to implement GDA so that it doesn't know anything about TSPs and can be used for every arbitrary optimizing method. That's why we

[3] *The selection of the abort criteria can be much more difficult for other problems. Consider the structure of a neuronal network, for example. The number of neurons and the number of the connections between the neurons will change all the time, even during a loop. In this case, there are no set numbers of which the criteria can consist.*

implement GDA as an abstract class that cannot instantiate itself.[4] We declare all problem-specific actions as abstract member functions, which are defined in the derived class. This way, we'll get a GDA implementation that can also be used to solve other problems. Take a look at the class declaration:

class Gda : public QObject

```
{
Q_OBJECT
public:
  Gda();
  virtual ~Gda();
  // This starts one run of GDA.
  // scaleFactor adjusts the rain speed to the scale of the
  // problem. qual is the initial quality of the problem.
  // loopLength tells GDA how long one loop through all
  // possibilities is.
  void startGda( DBL scaleFactor, DBL qual, int loopLength );

  // This stops a running calculation. Must be implemented
  // by derived classes.
  virtual void stop() = 0;

signals:
  // All these signals are meant for the GUI. They provide
  // information about the internal state of GDA.
  // The GUI may or may not
  // display them.
  void quality( double qual );
  void actions( int act );
  void accepted( int accep );
  void better( int bet );
  void rejected( int rej );
  void worseAccepted( int wor );

protected:
  // Since GDA doesn't know anything about the real problem
  // the next three member functions have to be implemented
  // as abstract members. The derived class that implements
  // the real problems has to implement them as well.
  virtual DBL nextAction() = 0;
  virtual void acceptAction() = 0;
  virtual DBL calcQuality() = 0;
```

continues ▶

[4] *A note to all C programmers who KDE got to take a closer look at C++: In C, this problem would be solved with Callback functions having a high rate of faults. In C++, an abstract class is written where some element functions are declared but not implemented. Other classes can be derived from such a base class and actually implement the abstract element functions. This way, the probability of a fault is much smaller because the compiler keeps the control over the type checking. Just because of that, it's worth writing programs in C++ rather than C!*

class Gda : public QObject continued

```
    // A flag that indicates that a running calculation
    // has been stopped.
    bool stopped;

  private:
    // Internal memeber functions.
    void loopComplete();
    void afterLoop();
    void evaluateAction( DBL qual );
    void adjustWaterLevel();
    DBL _waterLevel;
    DBL _quality;
    DBL _rainFactor;
    DBL _rainMin;
    int _actions;
    int _accepted;
    int _better;
    int _rejected;
    int _loopLength;
    bool _changed;
    bool _finished;
  };
```

The class `Gda` doesn't contain a screen representation; it's a pure workhorse (so to speak) drudging on in the background. That's why it's not derived from one of the Qt or KDE widgets. Because we want to use the signal-slot mechanism of Qt, we derive it from `QObject`. There's nothing interesting with the constructor and destructor.[5]

The functionality of `startGda()` hasn't been implemented in the constructor. We don't want `Gda` to immediately start after the creation. We want to explicitly be able to control the start and reuse `Gda`. The parameters passed `startGda()` are self-explanatory, except perhaps `scaleFactor`. The speed of how fast it rains in the solution space has to be adjusted to the level of magnitude of the TSP's quality. If it were to rain the same speed for all TSPs, our algorithm would stop too early in a TSP in the region of 0.0–1.0, but would take unnecessarily long when points are distributed over an edge length of 10000.0. We just use the diagonal of the rectangle where the points are in as the scaling factor.

The member function `stop()` enables the user to abort the optimization at any time. This possibility should always be given to the GUI user.

[5] *Another tip for the C++ newbies: Unless there is a good reason not to, it definitely makes sense to declare the destructor of the base class as virtual. This ensures that the whole cascade of destructors is called with derived classes as well and avoids many, at the first look, unexplainable memory leaks.*

Next we see six Qt signals. After every cycle of all changing possibilities for all points (I'll call this a "loop" from now on), GDA sends these signals. They provide information about the number of changes that have been tried, the number of accepted changes, the number of the ones that actually have been better, and so on. Furthermore, information relating to the level of quality reached thus far is provided. The GUI part of the program can receive these signals and display them in a suitable way for the user or it can just ignore them. It doesn't matter for the class `Gda` at all. It'll send the signals and doesn't care about whether the slots are actually connected with them.

In conventional environments—no matter whether C or C++—insecure Callback functions would have to serve for this. Qt frees the programmer from this nightmare and KDE extends this bonus to the KDE programmer (because KDE is based on Qt).

The next three member functions are all abstract declarations. The GDA algorithm has to induce the next change of our TSP, but it doesn't know that it is a TSP. This contradiction is solved by declaring the method `nextAction()`, but not implementing it. It is already used by the definition of the class `Gda`. To avoid anything going wrong, make sure that no instance can be created from `Gda` by using the `=0` at the end of the declaration. Derived classes have to take care of the implementation. The return value of `nextAction()` is the difference between the old and the new quality level and that's all `Gda` is interested in. The algorithm takes care of qualities of solutions only. How this quality gets calculated is not of interest. It's similar with `acceptAction()` and `calcQuality()`. After GDA has decided whether a change has an acceptable quality or whether it has to be rejected, TSP will have to induce exactly this: accept the change or reject it. Rejecting is easy. Because only the quality has so far been calculated after the call of `nextAction()` but nothing has really changed, it's enough to do nothing. It's different in the case of accepting. The data structure that represents the TSP internally has to be changed. The class `Gda` induces the derived class to do this by calling `acceptAction()`.

The rest of the declaration contains some internal data and methods needed internally and is not relevant to this discussion. Some details are of interest to us, however.

```
void Gda::startGda( DBL scaleFactor, DBL qual, int loopLength )
{
DBL diff;
  // There's no theoretical reason for these two values.
  // They are completely heuristic.
```

continues ▶

void Gda::startGda(DBL scaleFactor, DBL qual, int loopLength)
{
DBL diff; continued

```
_rainFactor = 1.0 / 500.0;
_rainMin = 0.01 * scaleFactor / 500.0;

_quality = qual;
_loopLength = loopLength;
_waterLevel = 1.2 * _quality;
_actions = _accepted = _better = _rejected = 0;
_finished = false;

// We call afterLoop() one time after having initialized
// all relevant internal variables in order to allow the
// GUI to display the
// initial information.
afterLoop();

// _finished will be set to "true" as soon as one
// whole loop has been performed without the occurrence
// of one single accepted change. In that
// case we stop GDA and declare the actual run as finished.

while ( !_finished )
  {
  // Before each loop we set the internal state to
  // "unchanged". If at least one change is accepted
  // _changed is set to "true".
  _changed = false;
  for ( int i = 0; i < _loopLength; i++ )
    {
    // nextAction() returns a quality difference "old - new"
    diff = nextAction();
    evaluateAction( _quality - diff );
    if ( stopped ) return;
    }
  loopComplete();
  }
}
```

You can see some initializations at the beginning; these are less interesting and pretty much self-explanatory. The *while* loop is the actual algorithm. We set the intern status to "unchanged" (`_changed = false`) at the beginning of each loop that is realized through the *for* loop so that we know whether something will have changed at the end of the loop.

Within the *for* loop, we call `nextAction()` for every possible change for every point. The returned quality difference is used to check with evaluateAction() as to whether the nextAction() proposed change is acceptable. After every loop, loopComplete() takes care of a few tasks (discussed soon).

Take a quick look at what evaluateAction() does:

void Gda::evaluateAction(DBL qual)

```
{
// Increase number of performed actions.
_actions++;
if ( qual >= _waterLevel )
  {
  // In case we reject this change we just increment the
  // number of rejected actions. Nothing else needs
  // to be done.
  _rejected++;
  }
else
  {
  if ( qual < _quality )
    {
    // Here we got a change that really improves the
    // quality.
    _better++;
    }
  // Whether the accepted change was really better
  // doesn't matter here. We just increment the
  // number of accepted changes.
  _accepted++;

  // We accept the new quality.
  _quality = qual;
  // Now it has to rain.
  adjustWaterLevel();

  // We accepted the change. Therefore we have to change
  // the internal state to "changed".
  _changed = true;

  // Here we tell the derived class that we accepted
  // the change. The derived class must decide what to
  // do with this information.
  acceptAction();
  }
}
```

In the case where the quality of the change is greater or equal to the water level, `Gda` rejects the change.[6] All other cases are acceptable. `Gda` distinguishes between "better" and "worse or acceptable" only for statistical tasks. It's not important for the function of the algorithm. `Gda` sets the internal quality corresponding to the returned value of `nextAction()`, lets it rain with `adjustWaterLevel()`, and calls `acceptAction()` so that the changes are affected.

As promised, there's `loopComplete()` left, which doesn't really do more than call `afterLoop()` at this stage.

void Gda::loopComplete()

```
{
// During one loop we deal only with quality differences. To
// allow GDA to adjust all the little inaccuracies we
// calculate the real quality once after each loop.
_quality = calcQuality();

// Let's allow KApplication to process some events in order
// to keep the GUI "responsive".
kapp->processEvents();

// We allow the GUI to catch up with the internal state.
afterLoop();

// If no changes have been accepted during the last loop
// we declare GDA as finished.
if ( !_changed )
  {
  _finished = true;
  }
}
```

During each loop, quality differences are constantly being calculated and added to or subtracted from our internal `_quality` variable. This leads to small inaccuracies that can add up over time. That's why we completely recalculate the quality after each loop. So, why don't we do this with every `nextAction()`? Simple answer: Because it takes longer than calculating only the difference of the qualities before and after each change. The member

[6] *Okay, okay. I admit that I lied a little bit. The cautious reader immediately noticed it and said, "Why greater or equal? It has always been said that the water level ascends slowly and that the quality has to stay on top of the water level!" Correct, that's what I talked about. The quality of a TSP actually will become better if the whole length of the circuit becomes smaller. That's why I just reversed the algorithm. We actually don't search for high summits in the solution space; we search instead for deep valleys. And the water level? How should I interpret that? Well, the whole description of mountains, valleys, plains, rain, and deluge is nothing more than a metaphor to simplify the imagination for us—obviously, our mental "pictures" should not be taken too literally.*

function `nextAction()` is called many hundred thousand times within the loop (in large problems, possibly even some million times). We should keep it as short as possible.

The line `kapp->processEvents()` is interesting. The method `startGda()` takes a long time before it returns. No other code is executed during this time, not even the part responsible for taking care of events (keyboard, mouse, and so on). The user clicks on a button and nothing happens. Such behavior (the nothing happening part) can't be tolerated in a GUI program. We have to give `KApplication` a chance, in between, to take care of some events. `KApplication` provides a global pointer `kapp` to make it easier for us.

This approach works because there can be only one instance of `KApplication` in every program. `KApplication` inherits the member function `processEvents()` from `QApplication`. This function takes care of events from the event queue for a maximum of three seconds or until no events are there anymore; it then returns. Three seconds are a horribly long time for a calculation-intensive program. We can rightfully assume, however, that unless the user hacks on the keyboard like crazy or makes a race with his mouse while he watches the program working, the function will never last three seconds.

Very distrusting programmers can use the function `processEvents( int maxtime )` instead; `maxtime` specifies in milliseconds how long the events can be worked off. *Warning:* If you ever get into a situation where you have to restrict the time for events, there is probably something wrong with your program (at least that's my opinion). After all, this means that events that have not yet been taken care of stay in the event queue. They'll stack up with time and the GUI will once more react only very hesitantly.

Programmer hint: If your program executes code for a long time without giving a chance to anything else to be executed, you'll have to call `kapp->processEvents()` from time to time; otherwise, the response characteristics of the GUI will be totally degenerated. The reason for this trouble is that Qt currently isn't "thread safe." We can only hope that future versions of Qt function safely with threads,[7] enabling us to run time-consuming operations in a thread other than the GUI. This would have other advantages, too: At the moment, no "blocking IO" is being performed. If an IO operation is blocked, the GUI is blocked, too. Because of this, we must execute all IO operations as "non-blocking," which is rather unpleasant.

[7] *The Trolls promised that!*

There's still `afterLoop()` left:

void Gda::afterLoop()

```
{
// Emit signals with the internal state of GDA to
// allow the GUI
// to catch up.
emit quality( _quality );
emit actions( _actions );
emit accepted( _accepted );
emit better( _better );
emit rejected( _rejected );
emit worseAccepted( _accepted - _rejected );
}
```

After every loop, `Gda` gives the GUI the possibility to provide the user with some refreshed indicators. `Gda` just sends the six signals that we talked about when we discussed the class declaration. The GUI can do whatever it wants with it, or even better, whatever we (the programmers) want.

3.4 It's Getting Concrete: *TspGda*

So far, we have finished the actual algorithm GDA and its implementation. We'll return to it when we write a dialog box that enables users to change some GDA internal parameters. Now it's time to take a look at the derived class `TspGda`, which converts the abstract class `Gda` into something from which we can actually create an instance.

Once again, here's the class declaration right at the beginning:

class TspGda : public Gda

```
{
Q_OBJECT

public:
  TspGda();
  ~TspGda();

signals:
  // All signals are for the GUI to catch up on
  // the progress of the optimization.
  void progressNeighbours( int number );
  void currentRun( int run );
  void bestRun( int bestRun );
  void bestQuality( double bestQuality );
  void tspReady( int bestRun );
  void statusChanged( int id );
  void pointsNumber( int number );
  void neighboursNumber( int number );

public slots:
```

```
  // Both slots start a TSP optimization. The first one
  // loads a provided TSP and optimizes it while the second
  // one generates a TSP and optimizes it (mostly for
  // testing purposes.)
  void startTsp( QString name, int iterations,
                 bool gen = false );
  void startTsp( int iterations );

protected:
  // Calculates the difference in quality of the current
  // course and of a small change of it
  // (oldQuality - newQuality) and returns difference.
  virtual DBL nextAction();
  // Changes the course according to nextAction().
  virtual void acceptAction();
  // Calculates the quality of the current course.
  virtual DBL calcQuality();

private:
  // The original course, either generated or loaded.
  Point *points;
  // The copy of points we are working on.
  Point *actualPoints;
  // The so far best course.
  Point *bestPoints;
  // An internal data structure which determines in which
  // sequence the points of a course are accessed.
  int *_access;
 // Some internal data,
 // deleted because uninteresting.
 // ...

};
```

I deleted a whole bunch of private data here from the source copy. That data would only blow it up unnecessarily and is irrelevant to your understanding of it. After the constructor and destructor, we see eight signals that are sent by `TspGda`; the GUI can use these signals to inform the user about the progress of the optimization.

Two slots, both called `startTsp()`, follow. They load a TSP from a hard disk or generate a random TSP for testing purposes. In the current version, 0.0.2, only the generating one is implemented. Later we'll get to loading and saving to the hard disk as well as over a network (including over the Internet). The optimization begins after the TSP is provided as a data structure.

The next three member functions—`nextAction()`, `acceptAction()`, `calcQuality()`—were discussed in the preceding section. Clearly, however, we'll take a closer look at the class definition.

The following three pointers all point to circuits in the TSP that we're working on: `points` points to the original circuit; `actualPoints` points to the current circuit; and `bestPoints` remembers the circuit that has had the best quality so far. For the program to have a practical use, it must be able to save the best result the optimization provides.

With regard to the data structure itself, it is an array that is practical because it makes the assignment of neighbors with the index really easy. On the other hand, we want to move quickly and without any problems through the circuit without making the computer calculate the addresses over and over again when we access the single points (`points[i]`). That's why every point contains both a pointer to the next one in the circuit and one to its predecessor. At the implementation, you'll see that the circuit with double pointers (which is actually in an array) makes very quick changes in the circuit possible.

There's the data structure `_access` left to discuss. Once again, I must confess: At the introduction of the Traveling Salesman Problem and the GDA algorithm, I said that the determination of the initial circuit for every GDA run is the only time when randomness is used. Experience has shown, however, that we can begin every run with the same initial circuit as long as we define another sequence in which all points of the circuits are being treated for each run. We don't directly access the single points with a counter variable. Instead, we access the points indirectly with the array `_access` containing the indices of all points in a random order.

Now, we're getting to the class definition, so let's first take a look at `startTsp()`:

void TspGda::startTsp(QString name, int iterations, bool gen)

```
{
stopped = false;
checkOldTsp();

if ( gen )
  {
  emit statusChanged( KTsp::STATUSBAR_GENERATING );
  points = io->generateTsp( 800, 10 );
  }
else
  {
  }

_numberOfPoints = io->numberOfPoints();
emit pointsNumber( _numberOfPoints );
_numberOfNeighbours = io->numberOfNeighbours();
emit neighboursNumber( _numberOfNeighbours );

if ( ( _numberOfPoints < 0 ) || ( _numberOfNeighbours < 0 ) )
```

```
    {
    cerr << "Not a valid TSP.\n";
    cerr << "Points = " << _numberOfPoints;
    cerr << " Neighbours = " << _numberOfNeighbours << "\n";
    exit (1);
    }

  emit statusChanged( KTsp::STATUSBAR_NEIGHBOURS );
  calcNeighbours();

  emit statusChanged( KTsp::STATUSBAR_OPTIMIZING );

  actualPoints = new Point[_numberOfPoints];
  CHECK_PTR( actualPoints );
  copyPoints( actualPoints, points );

  bestPoints = new Point[_numberOfPoints];
  CHECK_PTR( bestPoints );
  copyPoints( bestPoints, points );

  _access = new int[_numberOfPoints];
  CHECK_PTR( _access );
  _bestQuality = calcQuality();

  _bestRun = 0;
  emit currentRun( 0 );
  emit bestRun( _bestRun );

  emit bestQuality( _bestQuality );
  calcScale();

  for ( int it = 0; it < iterations; it++ )
    {
    emit currentRun( it + 1 );
    actPoint = 0;
    actNeighbour = 0;
    copyPoints( actualPoints, points );

    for ( int i = 0; i < _numberOfPoints; i ++ )
      {
      _access[i] = i;
      }

    for ( int i = 0; i < 10 * _numberOfPoints; i++ )
      {
      int temp;
      long i1, i2;

      i1 = rand->lrand( 0, _numberOfPoints - 1);
      i2 = rand->lrand( 0, _numberOfPoints - 1);
      temp = _access[i1];
      _access[i1] = _access[i2];
      _access[i2] = temp;
      }
```

continues ▶

void TspGda::startTsp(QString name, int iterations, bool gen) continued

```
  startGda( scaleFactor, calcQuality(), _numberOfPoints *
        _numberOfNeighbours

  if ( stopped ) return;
  DBL tempQuality = calcQuality();

  if ( tempQuality < _bestQuality )
    {
    _bestQuality = tempQuality;
    copyPoints( bestPoints, actualPoints );
    _bestRun = it + 1;
    emit bestRun( _bestRun );
    emit bestQuality( _bestQuality );
    }
  }
emit statusChanged( KTsp::STATUSBAR_READY );
emit tspReady( _bestRun );
}
```

First, the method sets the internal state of `TspGda` to "not stopped," and then uses `checkOldTsp()` to delete a possibly still-existing old TSP so we don't create a memory leakage. The next step is to let the class `TspIO` load or generate a TSP (only generating is implemented so far). A whole bunch of uninteresting initializations follow. Some of them take some time—the calculation of the nearest neighbors to each point, for example. In the meantime, `TspGda` sends signals from time to time to give the GUI a chance to inform the users about the progress.

A first approach would be to check whether it's worth connecting every point with every other point. A loop through all possibilities would be very long and our program would calculate for a long time. After some consideration, we determine that it is extremely unlikely that a connection with a point that is far away leads to a good quality. Experience has shown that it's normally enough to take the 10 nearest neighbors into account (which is actually hard coded at the moment). To give the user more flexibility, we'll make this customizable through a dialog box in a later exercise. For now, it's enough that the method `calcNeighbours()` determines the nearest neighbors and passes them to every point.

The interesting part begins at the first *for* loop. First we shuffle `_access` for every run and call `startGda()`. The method returns after a run has been completed. It is left to `TspGda` to calculate the total length of the resulting circuit. If it's smaller than the current best result, the current circuit is declared as the best and the next run begins. As always, `TspGda` sends signals to the GUI from time to time.

The most interesting methods are `nextAction()` and `acceptAction()`. Let's begin with `nextAction()`:

DBL TspGda::nextAction()

```
{
int actP = _access[actPoint];
Point *cpPointer = &(actualPoints[actP]);
Point *cpnPointer = cpPointer->nextPointer();
Point *cnPointer = &(actualPoints[cpPointer->neighbour( actNeighbour)]);
Point *cnnPointer = cnPointer->nextPointer();

DBL tempX = cpPointer->x() - cpnPointer->x();
DBL tempY = cpPointer->y() - cpnPointer->y();
DBL oldPart = sqrt( tempX * tempX + tempY * tempY );

tempX = cnPointer->x() - cnnPointer->x();
tempY = cnPointer->y() - cnnPointer->y();
oldPart += sqrt( tempX * tempX + tempY * tempY );
tempX = cpPointer->x() - cnPointer->x();
tempY = cpPointer->y() - cnPointer->y();
DBL newPart = sqrt( tempX * tempX + tempY * tempY );
tempX = cpnPointer->x() - cnnPointer->x();
tempY = cpnPointer->y() - cnnPointer->y();

newPart += sqrt( tempX * tempX + tempY * tempY );
oldPoint = actPoint++;
oldNeighbour = actNeighbour;


if ( actPoint >= _numberOfPoints )
  {
  actPoint = 0;
  oldNeighbour = actNeighbour++;
  if ( actNeighbour >= _numberOfNeighbours ) actNeighbour = 0;
  }
return oldPart - newPart;
}
```

Several pointers are initialized first: `cpPointer` points to the point that we're currently working on; `cpnPointer` points to the next point that the current one is connected to; `cnPointer` points to the current neighbor of our point; and `cnnPointer` points to the next points that the neighbor is connected to. Confusing?

Okay, Let's imagine the whole thing:

A->B->C->D->E->F->

F is connected with A. If B is our current point (`cpPointer`), C is the next point that B is connected to (`cpnPointer`). E is the current neighbor (`cnPointer`) to B, and F is the next point that E is connected to (`cnnPointer`).

Now we cut the course between B and C on the one side and E and F on the other side. Those are old connections. The method `nextAction()` calculates the sum of the old connections as `oldPart`. The new connections are between B and E on the one side and C and F on the other side. The sum of the lengths of those connections is `newPart`. The return value of `nextAction()` is `oldPart   newPart`. Notice that `nextAction` doesn't really change anything in the circuit but calculates just the lengths of some connections.

It's a little bit more difficult with `acceptAction()`, which really has to change the circuit:

void TspGda::acceptAction()

```
{
int cpIndex, cnIndex;
int cpnIndex, cnnIndex;
Point *cpPointer, *cnPointer;
Point *cpnPointer, *cnnPointer;
// First we we initialize some indeces and pointers with:
// cp[Index¦Pointer]        - the current point
// cpn[Index¦Pointer]       - the next point to the current point
// cn[Index¦Pointer]        - the current neighbour
// cnn[Index¦Pointer]       - the next point to the current neighbour
cpIndex = _access[oldPoint];
cpPointer = &(actualPoints[cpIndex]);
cpnIndex = cpPointer->nextIndex();
cpnPointer = cpPointer->nextPointer();
cnIndex = cpPointer->neighbour( oldNeighbour );
cnPointer = &(actualPoints[cnIndex]);
cnnIndex = cnPointer->nextIndex();
cnnPointer = cnPointer->nextPointer();

// If actual point and actual neighbour are directly after
// (or before) each other in the course the new course would
// duplicate the old one,but our data structure would
// become corrupted. So we stop here in this case.
if ( ( cpnIndex == cnIndex ) || ( cnnIndex == cpIndex ) )
    return;

// Now we cut apart the old connections and build the new
// ones. First new connection: cpIndex -> cnIndex. This one
// must be done with the direction.
cpPointer->setNextPointer( cnPointer );
cpPointer->setNextIndex( cnIndex );

// Next connection: cpnIndex -> cnnIndex. This one must be
// done against the direction.
cpnPointer->setLastPointer( cnnPointer );
cpnPointer->setLastIndex( cnnIndex );

// Next connection: cnnIndex -> cpnIndex. This one must
// also be done against the direction.
cnnPointer->setLastPointer( cpnPointer );
cnnPointer->setLastIndex( cpnIndex );

// Last connection: cnIndex -> cpIndex. This one must be
// done with the direction again.
```

```
cnPointer->setNextPointer( cpPointer );
cnPointer->setNextIndex( cpIndex );

// All new connections are done. Now we have to invert the
// direction of one of the two part of our course. It would
// be good if we could know (or even make a good guess)
// which is the shorter one.
// Unfortunately we don't know any efficient algorithm to
// find that out.
// If someone knows one drop us a note. For the time being
// we always choose the same one: cpnIndex up to cnIndex
// (including them).
Point *tmp;

do {
  tmp = cpnPointer->nextPointer();
  cpnPointer->flipDirection();
  cpnPointer = tmp;
  } while ( cpnPointer != cnPointer );

// That leaves just the last direction to invert.
cpnPointer->flipDirection();

// So ENIAC agrees, everything is done!
}
```

The comments already explain what is happening here. First, some pointers are initialized again. `cpPointer`, `cpnPointer`, `cnPointer`, and `cnnPointer` have the same meanings as they did in `nextAction()`. In addition, this time we need the indices of the involved points, too; those are `cpIndex`, `cpnIndex`, `cnIndex`, and `cnnIndex`. The meanings correspond to the pointers' meanings. If these meanings aren't clear to you, refer back to the preceding discussion about `nextAction()`.

If the current point and the current neighbor are situated directly before or after each other in the circuit, our action would reproduce the current circuit. This is not too bad, but we would destroy the internal data structure. To avoid this, the *if* statement will terminate the action immediately.

The following eight lines (pure source, no comments) cut the connections in the same manner as discussed earlier with regard to `nextAction()`, and create the new connections. Our circuit now looks like this:

A->B->E<-D<-C<-F->

You might be thinking, 'Hey, that doesn't look like a circuit.' Well, you're exactly right. Here's where the fact that we don't just deal with a ring of points comes into play. Our traveling salesman (or the drilling machine) actually moves from one point to the next. This means the connections have a direction. If we cut connections and create new ones, one part of the circuit will have false directions. The directions have to be reversed either in the part F->A->B->E or in the part E<-D<-C<-F. The do-loop, which follows in `acceptAction()`, takes care of this task. Fortunately, our data structure has double pointers.

`Point::flipDirection()` doesn't do anything except flip a `bool` variable in every point, determining which of the two pointers means "forward" and which means "backward."

Although it sounds strange, `TspGda` is in the small do-loop most of the time (like from 500 points on).

That's why it makes sense to optimize the loop as much as possible. It's already quite fast because of the double pointers. If it were possible to know which branch was the shorter one, the loop (and with it the whole program) performance would be enhanced. The source code comments say it all: I couldn't come up with a solution. But even if we would only guessed right 70% of the time, the speed increase would still be significant.

The following approach is conceivable: The branch that goes from the current point to the current neighbor is probably the shorter one in a halfway optimized TSP because it's not likely that it leads through many points. Although this statement is correct, it's of no use to us. Most of the accepted changes—and with them, calls of `acceptAction()`—happen at the beginning when the circuit isn't even anywhere close to "halfway optimized."[8] (In fact, it's really in a pretty bad state at that point.) That's why the preceding statement is right for a few changes at the end of a run only. If a reader knows a codable answer to this problem, I would be very interested in it!

3.5 Adaptations In the Class KTsp

Before dealing with the GUI part of KTsp, we should take a look at version 0.0.2. From the files on the New Riders website, install ktsp-0.0.2.tgz:

```
tar -xzvf ktsp-0.0.2.tgz
cd ktsp-0.0.2
./configure
make
make install
```

For the last step, you must have root rights.

[8] *If you watch the program during optimization, you'll notice that it seems to become faster at the end. (This is the reason for the speed-up.)*

Now start the new version of KTsp. You'll see a window just like the one shown in Figure 3.1. A new menu point has been added and a new icon has been added to the toolbar. Some indicators now fill the previously empty KTsp windows. The status bar is split in half and doesn't just show "Ready"; it actually shows useful information about the status of the program. Don't worry about the "plain" look of KTsp just yet. We'll spruce it up a bit later. At the moment, our focus is on the core functionality, and the current look is a just a compromise that enables us to see what the program does.

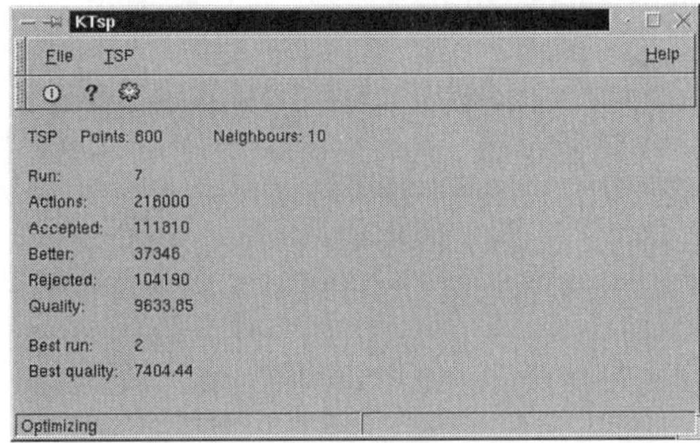

Figure 3.1 *KTsp at work.*

The class declaration of KTsp had to be expanded to get along with the new information. You can see this because many QLabels have been instantiated within KTsp. They show all the relevant data about the progress of the optimization. Furthermore, some slots[9] that receive signals from our calculation slave `TspGda` have been added. Another innovation is that KTsp now creates an instance of `TspGda`. It's not worth showing the class declaration at this point. (If you are interested in taking a look at it, review the source code; it should be clear with your current knowledge.) Instead, let's take a look at some source snippets from the class definition.

We want to use some QLabels as an example:

```
actions = new QLabel( i18n( "Actions:" ), w );
CHECK_PTR( actions );
actions->setGeometry( 10, 60, 70, 20 );

actions_num = new QLabel( "", w );
```

[9] *The names of all slots in the program begin with the prefix* SLOT. *This is not mandatory; it's just a convention that I have gotten used to. You can't know whether something is a slot within a *.C file without taking a look in the *.h file. That's why I use this particular prefix.*

```
CHECK_PTR( actions_num );
actions_num->setGeometry( 90, 60, 70, 20 );
connect( tsp, SIGNAL( actions( int ) ),
         actions_num, SLOT( setNum( int ) ) );
```

Both the QLabels show the number of actions that have been performed during the optimization. The first one, `actions`, is a static QLabel to which we just assign the text it's supposed to display. We internationalize the text with `i18n()` and prepare it for localization (translation). The second QLabel, `actions_num`, is more interesting. With the help of `connect()`, we connect it with the Signal `actions()`, which is sent by `TspGda`. That's all we have to do to guarantee that the current number of actions sent by the calculation slave will display.

Lazy programmers will like the second parameter that we pass along to the constructor of QLabel. It is a pointer to the parent widget. Child widgets are automatically deleted if the parent widget is deleted. In other words, we don't have to bother with deleting all child widgets in the destructor of the parent widget. Qt automatically takes care of that for us. This property of Qt and KDE—which KDE inherits from Qt—prevents tons of memory leakage creating possibilities!

All widgets provided by Qt, just like all widgets of KDE, have this property. We need only to specify a parent, because the constructor will specify `parent = 0` if we don't do it. Unless specified, widgets don't know a parent and so there is no automatic deletion.

All widgets contain a member function called `setGeometry( x, y, w, h)`. `x` and `y` are the coordinates of the upper-left corner of the widget relative to the parent widget. Width and height can be adjusted over `w` and `h`. The layout management discussion examines more (and better) ways to adjust widget geometry.

QLabel contains the slots `setNum( int )` and `setNum( double )`, which make it possible to connect the QLabel `actions_num` directly. This means that the QLabel can frequently change its content upon receipt of a signal from `TspGda`. This feature is realized in the line where `connect()` is called. Whenever `TspGda` sends a new value, `actions_num` automatically displays it—a fine thing, which eases the work of the programmer significantly.

The counterpart to `connect()` is `disconnect()`, which can break a connection between signals and slots. You call disconnect only if you don't want the signal to be received anymore (which would be very seldom). When either the object that sends the signal or the object that receives the signal gets deleted, you don't have to break the connection explicitly with `disconnect()` (although it's up to you whether you want to). Qt automatically takes care of this task for you.

Unfortunately, there's no possibility of specifying the number of digits or precision for `QLabel::setNum( double )`.

We can achieve this, however, in two ways:

1. We can add a slot to KTsp that receives the signal, converts it to a string, and later calls `QLabel::setText()`.
2. We can derive our own class `MyLabel` from QLabel which would contain a slot that takes care of both the conversion and formatting, and internally calls `setText()`.

This can be done, but I thought it would be too much work for our compromise GUI (which will be exchanged for a better one anyway). The trailing digits of the quality surely aren't that interesting.

All other QLabel pairs are so created: The static QLabel just gets the text assigned, and the dynamic one is connected to a slot.

The statusbar is another point of interest:

void KTsp::setupStatusbar()

```
{
// A statusbar with two entries.
statusbar()->insertItem( "A very long text which will"
                         "be replaced asap." , 0 );
statusbar()->changeItem( i18n( "Waiting for user" ), 0 );
statusbar()->insertItem( "                        ", 1 );
}
```

With `statusbar->insertItem()`, we create two items in the status bar. Because the command also specifies the length of the item, we just pass a long text. For the item with the ID 0, this is just a very long sentence that we don't prepare for the translation with `i18n()` because it will never really get displayed anyway. The text is actually immediately changed with `statusbar->changeItem()` to `"Waiting for user"`; we'll prepare this text for the translation. Later, both items can be accessed with ID 0 or 1.

```
connect( tsp, SIGNAL( statusChanged( int ) ),
         this, SLOT( slotStatusChanged( int ) ) );
```

This command connects the signal `statusChanged()` in `TspGda` with the slot `slotStatusChanged()` in KTsp. The slot will be as follows:

void KTsp::slotStatusChanged(int id)

```
{
// Change statusbar according to internal state
switch( id )
  {
  case STATUSBAR_READY:
```

continues ▶

void KTsp::slotStatusChanged(int id) continued

```
      statusbar()->changeItem( i18n( "Ready" ), 0 );
      break;

    case STATUSBAR_WATING:
      statusbar()->changeItem( i18n( "Waiting for user" ), 0 );
      break;

    case STATUSBAR_GENERATING:
      statusbar()->changeItem( i18n( "Generating TSP" ), 0 );
      break;

    case STATUSBAR_NEIGHBOURS:
      statusbar()->changeItem( i18n( "Generating neighbours" ), 0 );
      break;

    case STATUSBAR_OPTIMIZING:
      statusbar()->changeItem( i18n( "Optimizing" ), 0 );
      break;

    default:
      statusbar()->changeItem( i18n( "Something is wrong" ), 0 );
      break;

    }
}
```

The slot changes the display in the status bar with `statusbar->changeItem()`, corresponding to the values defined in an enumeration. The beauty is that there's no special cost involved in making the GUI react to the changes of the calculation slave `TspGda`. `TspGda` doesn't have to make any assumptions about the GUI. It doesn't even have to know whether there'll actually be something that reacts to the signals. The signal-slots mechanism makes this possible.

3.6 A Short Tour of Some of the Help Classes

`TspIO` is a fairly simple class at the moment. All it can do so far is randomly create a TSP and return it to the caller. It'll become more complex over the course of time. As soon as it can load and save TSPs, we'll take a close look at it (because we'll use the functionality of Qt). The next step is to create network-transparent IO operations. `TspIO` will teach the KDE mechanism how to use FTP.

We'll take a close look at this, too. Finally, we'll implement drag and drop. It's not worth bogging ourselves down in the details just yet, however.

Random is the other help class that we use. It is totally independent of Qt and KDE. I'll leave it by thanking Makoto Matsumoto and Takuiji Nishimimura for developing this extremely fast algorithm, which provides very good random numbers. Faults in the implementation—if there are any—are my fault and my fault alone.

Why not use `rand()` or `drand48()`? In "Numeric Recipes in C" the authors advise everyone not to use rand() since it's supposed to be implemented rather badly on various systems. When I began to use the DEC Alpha, `drand48()` provided anything else but random numbers. The problem is fixed now—at least, it seems to be fixed. Otherwise, Random exists now. It can be expanded very well to generate normally distributed random numbers, for example, and it generates very good random numbers very fast. That's why I decided not to throw it away, but to reuse it. The algorithm itself is not of interest for this book and I won't get into details.

3.7 Why Not Another Design?

After introducing signals and slots, a new question arises: Why haven't we used a completely different design for our program. `Gda` and `Tsp` could be two totally different classes that communicate over signals and slots. `Tsp` sends a signal that contains the next action. `Gda` answers the signal and either rejects or accepts it. It would be a much more elegant design! Right?

The short answer is, "It wouldn't work." The detailed answer is a little bit longer. If a signal is sent, Qt will make sure that the slot connected to the signal is called just like a normal function. Program control won't return to where the signal has been sent from before the slot's execution has finished. In other words, if we send a signal, we actually call a function, the slot. The difference is that Qt makes sure that everything is working if there's no slot.

This presents no problem so long as we're in the GUI. Because the user just clicks on several buttons, menu items, or icons, we'll never really get more than a few slots deep. If our calculation slaves, `Tsp` and `Gda`, would communicate over signals and slots, slots would call other slots, which would again call other slots. This could happen many hundred thousand times or even a million times without the program control returning to the starting point. Because we don't have an unlimited stack, our program will crash sooner or later. The following mini-program demonstrates the problem:

```
#include <qobject.h>
class Foo : QObject
  {
  Q_OBJECT
  signals:
    void send();
  public slots:
    void receive();
  };

Foo::receive()
```

```
    {
    emit send();
    }

  int main()
    {
    Foo *a = new Foo;
    Foo *b = new Foo;

    connect( a, SIGNAL( send() ), b, SLOT( received() ) );
    connect( b, SIGNAL( send() ), a, SLOT( received() ) );
    a->receive();
    return 0;
    }
```

Compile the program and please don't forget to link it against the Qt library and X library. Now start it. Depending on the speed of your computer and the size of the virtual memory (RAM plus swap space), it will run a short time and end in a core dump. The slots call each other without a break, which leads to a stack overflow. Similar things—just with a few more signals and slots—would happen if `Gda` and `Tsp` were to communicate over the signal-slot mechanism.

If you want to use signals and slots for objects other than GUI elements, you must carefully think about what really happens in your program. Forget the signals, but think about slots (which call each other). That's how you get a clue as to whether the program will lead to stack problems. *My personal caveat:* Don't use it at all!

3.8 Display the Result Graphically

The GUI of our program is still kind of plain. The user sees some quickly changing numbers and that's all. It's not really state-of-the-art comfort, is it? The user naturally wants the results to display graphically. Now that we've finished the core of the application, we must take care of the graphical output of the data.

Before we take a look at the source code, install ktsp-0.0.3 (the next version of our program). You can find it on the New Riders website. The installation is the same as previous installations.

If you start the program, you'll see a new menu item, View (see Figure 3.2). Click on it and three menu entries will display, each of which are gray. That means they're not activated. The user can click on them, but nothing will happen. It works this way because no TSP exists in the program yet, so they cannot be displayed. Now start TSP by selecting TSP, New TSP from the menu or with the gear in the toolbar. After a short time, after TSP has been created, the three items change to black. Now they're activated and can be used.

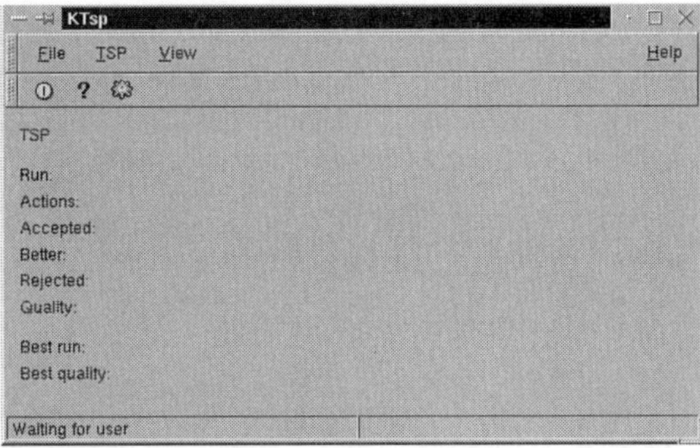

Figure 3.2 *A new menu item: View.*

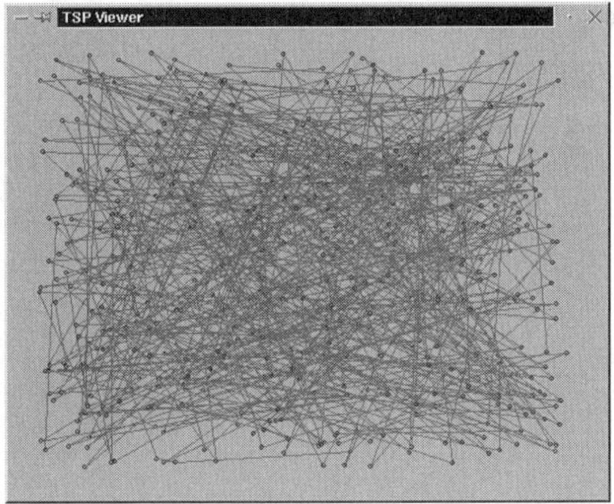

Figure 3.3 *A freshly generated TSP.*

Before we focus on the details of the program changes, play around with the three view possibilities. Show Best TSP displays the current best solution. This is the first item because I think that the user is especially interested in it. Show Original TSP displays the TSP that has been created (or later, loaded). Show Current TSP displays the TSP that is currently being worked on (the exact state of the optimization at the moment when the menu item is clicked).

Users can open as many view windows as they want, although the desktop might become rather confusing after a short time. The TSP viewer doesn't have its own menu. Although possible, it's rather useless because the only possible interaction would be to close the window. The "X" in the title bar takes care of this.

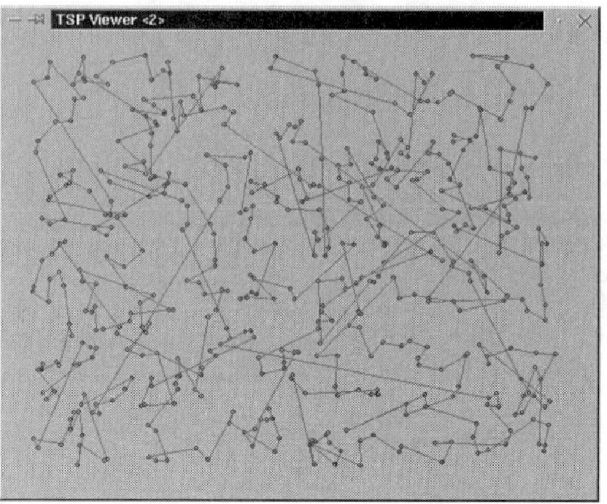

Figure 3.4 *A halfway optimized TSP.*

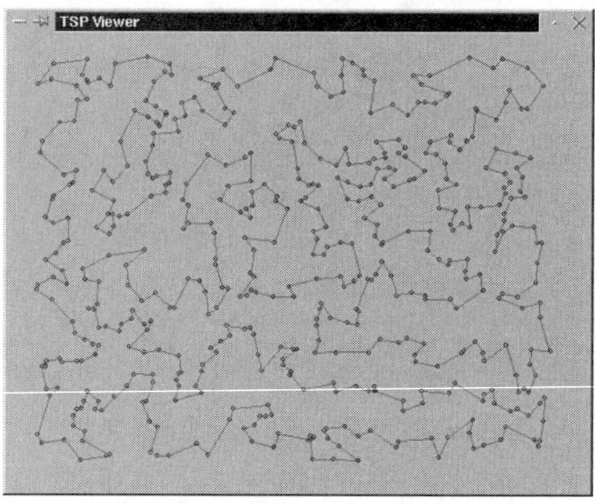

Figure 3.5 *An optimized TSP.*

It's time to take a look at the source code to see how the task has been accomplished. At the beginning, we derive our own widget from the QWidget called Canvas, where the actual drawing will be performed. The class declaration is rather simple:

class Canvas : public QWidget

```
{
public:
  Canvas( QWidget *parent = 0, const char *name = 0 );
  virtual ~Canvas();
  void setPoints( Point *tsp );
  void setParameters( DBL w, DBL h, DBL mx, DBL my );
```

```
protected:
  virtual void paintEvent( QPaintEvent *e );

private:
  QPixmap *pixmap;
  Point *points;
  DBL _width;
  DBL _height;
  DBL _marginX;
  DBL _marginY;
};
```

The constructor contains two parameters: parent and name. If they're not specified at the call of the constructor, the default value 0 is assigned to them. As already said, `name` is used only for internal debugging purposes. It's different with the parameter parent. If a parent widget is specified, the lazy programmer doesn't have bother with deleting the child widgets. Their deletion happens automatically upon deletion of their parent widget.

The only really interesting thing in the class Canvas is the virtual member function `paintEvent()`. Every QWidget, every KDE widget, and every other derived widget inherits this member function.

The method will be called if the widget has to be redrawn. Because it's declared as virtual, we can overwrite it in Canvas and let it draw whatever we want to. We'll use it to graphically display TSP.

Take a look at the implementation of `paintEvent()`:

*void Canvas::paintEvent(QPaintEvent *)*

```
{
if ( points != 0 )
  {
  QRect r = rect();

  if ( pixmap == 0 )
    {
    pixmap = new QPixmap( r.size() );
    pixmap->fill( this, r.topLeft() );
    Point *p = points;
    QPainter *painter = new QPainter( pixmap );
    CHECK_PTR( painter );
    painter->setWindow( _marginX, _marginY,
                _width, _height);
    painter->setViewport( 10, 10, width() - 20,
                height() - 20 );

    do
      {
      painter->setPen( blue );
```

continues ▶

*void Canvas::paintEvent(QPaintEvent *)* continued

```
        painter->drawArc( p->x() - 2, p->y() - 2, 4, 4,
                    0, 16*360 );
        painter->setPen( red );
        painter->drawLine( p->x(), p->y(),
                    p->nextPointer()->x(),
                    p->nextPointer()->y() );
        p = p->nextPointer();
        } while( p != points );

      delete painter;
      bitBlt( this, r.topLeft(), pixmap );
      }
    else
      {
      bitBlt( this, r.topLeft(), pixmap );
      }
    }
}
```

The first thing we notice is that `paintEvent( QPaintEvent * )` doesn't assign a name to the parameter. The reason is simple: The method doesn't use this parameter. Some compilers will answer with some annoying warnings; we can avoid these, however, by specifying the type of the parameter, but not the parameter itself.

If you get such warnings in your own project, remember that you can avoid them by leaving out the parameter (not the type!) in the definition.

In the declaration of Canvas, you can see that there's a member function `setPoints()`, which passes a TSP to Canvas. Before, the constructor sets the internal pointer `points`, which points to a TSP to 0. The method `paintEvent()` checks first whether `points` really points to data. If it doesn't point to data, the method won't do anything. Otherwise, a paint event could take place before Canvas actually contains data. It would end in a core dump because Canvas would try to access non-existing data with a null pointer.

After the method determines the size of our widget with `rect()`, it checks whether there has already been a QPixmap with the drawing. If there hasn't been one, it creates a QPixmap with the right size and fills it with the background of the widget Canvas. The next step is to create a QPainter that can draw on QWidgets and QPixmaps. Over `setWindow()` and `setViewport()`, QPainter can be set to automatically map the coordinates of our points to the size of the widget, and the actual drawing begins. The *do* loop goes through every TSP point and draws a little blue circle for every point as well as a red line as the connection to the next point. QPainter is deleted afterward because it's no longer needed, and the QPixmap is copied into the widget with `bitBlt()`.

If there's an already existing QPixmap, `paintEvent()` doesn't do anything except just copy it to the Canvas.

Why this approach? The first reason is that we have to draw the graphic only one time, at the first call of `paintEvent()` at which data already exists. The drawing takes a lot longer than the copying. We save time, which we can use for further optimizations in the program. The second reason is of an aesthetic nature. Let's say that we draw the graphic every time directly on the Widget. If that were the case, we would have to erase the old graphic first and draw the new one. That would lead to a lot of flicker, if many redraw requests follow each other. There's a lot less flicker by copying the QPixmap into the Canvas because we don't have to erase anything. We buy speed and aesthetics for the memory of the additional QPixmap. I think that it's worth it.

After the `paintEvent()` is clear, we need to take a look at the tools that are used.

QRect isn't anything special. Just like the names says, it's a class that defines a rectangle. It can be passed along to functions as a parameter or it can be returned by functions.

QPixmap is more exciting. Actually, it can be imagined as a rectangular piece of the screen which doesn't display itself onscreen. You can copy from an appropriately sized piece of a widget into a QPixmap and the other way round, but it's more than a passive cache. You can draw in it just like with the screen, which makes it practical for every task for which you have to invisibly finish the graphic first and then display the whole thing at once.

QPainter is a powerful tool. It's important to us because we can use it to paint and write on QWidgets, QPixmaps, and QPrinter (a logical printing device). Besides drawing points, QPainter can be used to draw lines, rectangles, ellipses, circles and circle segments, pie graphics, polygons, Bézier functions, and some other things such as whole pictures (QPicture), and naturally, text. The methods begin with the word *draw* and have logical names: `drawEllipse()` draws an ellipse; `drawPolygon()` draws a polygon. The other methods are named accordingly. Different line widths, pen styles (lines, dotted lines, and so on), and colours belong to its repertoire, too.

In our `paintEvent()`, these two lines are important:

```
painter->setWindow( _marginX, _marginY, _width, _height);
painter->setViewport( 10, 10, width() - 20, height() - 20 );
```

The widget Canvas has a specific size. Let's say it is 500 pixels wide and 400 pixels high. The TSP has a totally different size, but the same aspect ratio (which has been taken care of at the creation of the instance of

Canvas). The points of the TSP could be in a rectangle with the origin at (0.0, 0.0) and which is 5000.0 wide and 4000.0 high. It doesn't matter whether the measurement is in millimeters or light years. It would be a pain to do the conversion of every point on our own. Actually, QPainter takes care of it for us. With `setWindow()`, we set the logical origin to be at `(_marginX, _marginY)`, which corresponds to the smallest X and Y values of the points; the logical width corresponds to the width of our TSP; and the logical height corresponds to the height of our TSP.

With `setViewport()`, we now set a 10-pixel-wide margin around the TSP. The parameters of `setWindow()` correspond to the logical origin and the logical width and height of the rectangle; the `setViewport()` parameters actually correspond to the actual widget and have to be given in pixel.

The explanation of this difference is a bit short in the Qt documentation and leads to misunderstandings from time to time.[10] From now on, we can use the coordinates of our TSP for the drawing operations and QPainter will automatically convert them into pixel coordinates.

Pay attention that, at least, the aspect ratio of the rectangle that contains everything that has to be drawn corresponds fairly with the aspect ratio of the widget. If that's not the case, circles will become ellipses and squares rectangles.

Besides this "view transformation" called *conversion*, QPainter also masters so-called *world transformations*, which enable rotations and shearings. Because we don't need them in our program, I don't want to get into details here. I nevertheless encourage you to take a look at the excellent Qt documentation, which can be directly used as online Help in the KDE File Manager (kfm) or the KDE Help system (kdehelp). QPainter details really are beyond the scope of this book.

QPainter can be used in two different ways: We can create an instance without specifying what we want to draw on; alternatively, we can pass a device right along to the constructor of QPainter. To create an instance of QPainter without specifying a drawing device, we must explicitly call the methods `begin()` and `end()`. Here's an example:

10 *To illustrate the difference, try to image it this way:* `setWindow()` *takes a rectangular cutting of the XY plane and fits it into the widget. For this, the function needs to know the real coordinates of the cutting and convert them into logical coordinates of the widget. However,* `setViewport()` *doesn't have to do anything with the XY plane. It only restricts the usable space of the widget. That's why the parameters have to be specified in pixel.*

QPainter painter;

```
painter.begin( this );
painter.setPen( black );
painter.drawPoint( x, y );
// some more drawings
painter.end();
```

In this case, we have to inform QPainter with `begin()` about the device we want to draw on and later break the connection between QPainter and the device with `end()`.

The other possibility is to pass the drawing device right along to the constructor of QPainter:

QPainter painter(this);

```
painter.setPen( black );
painter.drawPoint( x, y );
// some more drawings
```

This constructor implicitly calls `begin()` and `end()`. I prefer the second method because I tend to forget the `end()` and I'm an exceptionally lazy programmer. Doubtlessly, the first way is more flexible. It makes it possible to connect QPainter to different devices in between.

Canvas inherits the method `bitBlt()` from QWidget. It copies rectangular cuttings from QWidgets and QPixmaps—that's about it.

A word about `paintEvent()` in general: Normally, we don't need to concern ourselves as to whether the member function will be called and when. The X server and Qt take care of that for us. In case it's necessary to explicitly force the widget to redraw, the member function `update()` can be called. (Every widget has this member function.) If data that has to be displayed is changed, for example, you can force the widget with `update()` to adjust its graphic.

Now we can leave Canvas and take a look at the other changes in our program. The most important one is the creation of another KTMainWindow (KTMW) or, even better, the derived class: View. The class declaration looks pretty simple and we actually don't need to add much to KTMW:

class View : public KTMainWindow

```
{
public:
  View();
  virtual ~View();
  void drawTsp( Point *tsp );
```

continues ▶

class View : public KTMainWindow continued

```
protected:
  void calcScale();

private:
  Canvas *w;
  Point *points;
  DBL _width;
  DBL _height;
  DBL _marginX;
  DBL _marginY;
};
```

The whole class declaration is mostly self-explanatory. This class is the TSP viewer that uses Canvas as its drawing board. The drawing begins with `drawTsp()`; `calcScale()` calculates the parameters necessary to adapt the aspect ratio of the window to the TSP one.

First, let's take a look at the constructor:

View::View()
: KTMainWindow()

```
{
// create the main widget of View
w = new Canvas( this, "View Display" );
CHECK_PTR( w );

// tell KTMW that w is the main widget
setView( w );

// Set a better title than "KTsp <2>"
setCaption( i18n( "TSP Viewer" ) );
}
```

Just like in KTsp (our other class derived from KTMW), View creates a widget first, which is declared as the main widget of KTMW with `setView()`. This time it's no instance of QWidget, but an instance of our own Canvas. The title of the window, which is displayed in the title bar, can be set with `setCaption()`. We prepare the title for translation with `i18n()`. Only `setCaption()` is new for us. That's why we now take a look at the function `drawTsp()`:

*void View::drawTsp(Point *tsp)*

```
{
if ( tsp == 0 )
  {
  // This can't happen because we enable the corresponding
  // menu entry only when there really is something to view.
```

```
    // We do this anyway, just in case ...
    KMsgBox box( this, i18n( "TSP Error" ),
                       i18n( "No TSP ready for displaying!" ),
                       KMsgBox::STOP,
                       i18n( "Dismiss" ) );
    box.exec();
    close();
    }
else
    {
    points = tsp;
    calcScale();
    w->setFixedSize( w->width(),
                     ( w->width() * _height ) / _width );
    w->setPoints( points );
    w->setParameters( _width, _height, _marginX, _marginY );
    updateRects();
    }
}
```

The first branch of the *if* statement is self-explanatory. This situation can't happen because the corresponding menu entries are deactivated until there is data. Still, someone else could possibly add a button to the toolbar later, which also calls this function, but forget to deactivate it as long as there's no data. In this case, we open a little message box with the corresponding message.

The class KMsgBox is really practical for short text. It can be automatically customized with symbols and buttons. Basically, it's a specialized dialog box that displays a message for the user but doesn't enable him to change anything. It is interesting that the dialog box isn't displayed with `show()`; it is displayed with `exec()`. This makes the dialog box modal and the user won't be able to continue with the application until the dialog box is closed. At the end, `close()` closes the window without terminating the program.

Normally, KTMW manages the size of its main widget. If KTMW changes the size, the main widget will be adjusted so that it fits exactly in the free space of KTMW. In this case, we want something else, however. We want the main widget (the instance of Canvas) to be adjusted to the size of our TSP and to force KTMW to adjust itself around the main widget.

We achieve this through `setFixedSize()`, a method that every widget inherits as well as `setFixedWidth()` and `setFixedHeight()`, whose names explain their functions. First `calcScale()` calculates how big the instance of Canvas has to be to display the TSP appropriately.

The resulting parameters are set by `setFixedSize()` as the size. KTMW still hasn't reacted, but with `updateRects()` it adjusts itself and considers the number of toolbars if they're inserted in the window or if they're floating on the desktop. For your own applications, you should bear in mind that KTMW—and all derived classes—normally define the size of your main widget; if the size of the main widget is fixed, however, KTMW will adjust to it.

There're only the relevant changes in KTsp left to be discussed. Most of them are changes in the constructor and four new slots. We don't need to show the whole class declaration for this. Let's take a look at the changes in the constructor:

```
// The View menu
// We need to access this menu and its entries later.
// Therefore we store the menu as well as the entry ids.
tspMenu = new QPopupMenu;
CHECK_PTR( tspMenu );

// Create a View menu
// and disable the entries because there isn't anything to
// view yet.
best_id = tspMenu->insertItem( i18n( "Show &Best TSP" ),
                  this,
                  SLOT( slotViewBestTsp() ) );
tspMenu->setItemEnabled( best_id, false );
orig_id = tspMenu->insertItem( i18n( "Show &Original TSP" ),
                  this, SLOT( slotViewOrigTsp() ) );
tspMenu->setItemEnabled( orig_id, false );
current_id = tspMenu->insertItem( i18n( "Show &Current TSP" ),
                   this,
                   SLOT( slotViewCurrentTsp() ) );
tspMenu->setItemEnabled( current_id, false );

// The View menu goes into the Menubar.
menuBar()->insertItem( i18n( "&View" ), tspMenu );
```

They only construct and insert the new menu, View. To activate the menu items later, must need to be able to access the menu and its entries. That's why we can't just forget the pointer to the menu and the IDs of the items as we did with the other menus.

At the beginning, we create the menu over a pointer that is part of the class and not of the constructor. Next, we insert the three menu items one after another and connect them with the slots `slotViewBestTsp()`, `slotViewOrigTsp()`, and `slotViewCurrentTsp()`, and deactivate them with the method `setItemEnabled()`. At the end, we insert the whole menu onto the menubar.

The three slots are all pretty simple:

void KTsp::slotViewOrigTsp()

```
{
viewTsp( ORIG_TSP );
}

void KTsp::slotViewCurrentTsp()
{
viewTsp( CURRENT_TSP );
}
```

void KTsp::slotViewBestTsp()

```
{
viewTsp( BEST_TSP );
}
```

void KTsp::viewTsp(int id)

```
{
// This looks like a memory leakage but isn't because View
// is a new KTMW.
display = new View();
CHECK_PTR( display );
display->show();
display->drawTsp( tsp->getPoints( id ) );
}
```

All three functions call `viewTsp()` with the corresponding ID. In `viewTsp()`, the new window derived from KTMW is created first and forced to appear onscreen with `show()`. The call of `View::drawTsp()` with the pointer to the correct TSP that is returned by `TspGda::getPoints()` is next.

If the user opens multiple TSP viewers, all of them will be created over the same pointer display, which looks like a perfect possibility to create a memory leakage. If the second viewer is created, there won't be a pointer to the first one anymore, which could be used to delete it and free the memory. At first sight, it really looks like it. After we've thought about it a bit, we'll see that there's indeed *no* memory leakage.

An instance of the class View is a KTMW. It doesn't have to be deleted "from the outside." It takes care of this by itself. This differs totally from a dialog box, for example. A click on buttons such as OK, Cancel, and so on in a dialog box will make the dialog box disappear from the screen, but the instance is still there and has to be explicitly freed if it has been created on the heap. If the programmer created it on the stack, it will naturally disappear by itself when the function is left. A KTMW, on the other hand, deletes itself and all child widgets when the window is closed. The memory that hasn't been freed by the child-parent mechanism of Qt is automatically freed so that we can be sure that there's no memory leakage.

If you still have ktsp-0.0.2 lying around, start an optimization and click on the X in the window title (do not select File, Quit). It will end in a core dump because the `TspGda` is still calculating while the data it is working on gets deleted. That's a bug which we didn't notice in the preceding version. Fortunately, there's a solution. KTMW always calls its own method `queryClose()` before it really closes itself. We've overwritten this member function:

```
bool KTsp::queryClose()
{
tsp->stop();
return true;
}
```

Before we allow KTMW to really close itself, we stop the calculation. Actually, `queryClose()` is meant to clean things up before the end. For example, changed data can be saved. This is useful for editors, and we'll use it later to save optimized TSPs. You can also abuse the method by returning false. In this case, the window will refrain from closing itself if the user clicks on the X in the title bar, but not if the user clicks on File, Quit. If you ask me, I don't know what the use is. I recommend to always return true, but to create first a state that makes a clean closing possible without losing data.

At the end of this chapter, one question remains: how do we activate the three entries on the menu? The slot `slotCoursesReady()` takes care of that:

void KTsp::slotCoursesReady()

```
{
// All three internal TSPs are initialized. We can enable
// the corresponding menu entries now.
// We don't need to disable them again because from now on
// there always are TSPs ready.
tspMenu->setItemEnabled( best_id, true );
tspMenu->setItemEnabled( orig_id, true );
tspMenu->setItemEnabled( current_id, true );
}
```

When `TspGda` initiates all three TSPs, or circuits—the original, the best, and the current—it sends the signal `coursesReady()`, which is connected with this slot in KTsp. The slot calls `setItemEnabled()` for every entry with the saved pointer to the menu View. The items will be activated and the users can take a look at the TSPs.

4

KTsp Becomes Configurable

So far, we have hard coded a couple of parameters in the source, including the number of TSP points (if it is to be generated), the number of neighbors, and the number of runs with which KTsp tries to optimize. The rain speed (do you still remember GDA?) is also hard coded in the source. Additionally, we could think about the colours that should be used for the points and lines in the TSP viewer. Some users might not like the circles that represent the points in the viewer.

We don't want to expect users to recompile KTsp if they want to change these parameters, and the same applies to the programmer who has to test the program under various conditions. The answer is: We need a configuration dialog box or even multiple ones, because some things don't relate to each other. The number of neighbors who have to be considered is specified at the same place where the number of points is specified. Actually, they don't have anything to do with each other. The number of points influences the number generator. The number of neighbors is a parameter that influences the optimizations, just like the amount of rainfall.

We can specify some groups of parameters that belong to each other as the following table shows.

Group	Parameters
TSP	Number of points
Optimization	Number of neighbors
	Number of runs
	Amount of rainfall
Graphics	Colour of the points
	Colour of the connections
	Line width of the connection lines
	Shape of the points
	Size of the points

That makes a decent collection. We should think about which changes can come into force immediately and which must take effect later. The number of the points can be considered only with the next TSP that is generated anyway. The number of neighbors could be taken into account at the next run of the current TSP.

To simplify the program, we want to activate this change with the next TSP only. The number of runs can be changed during an optimization without any problem. If the number should be less than the runs that have already taken place, the optimization will just quit after the current run. A change of the rainfall speed can be done even during a run. The graphics parameter will activate only at the opening of a new TSP viewer anyway, because we draw in a TSP viewer only once. After that we just copy.

Last, but not least, we have to think about the design of the dialog box(es). Many developers prefer tabbed dialog boxes. You can find a good example of one in the DVI viewer (kdvi) by clicking on Options, Preferences. This dialog box's compact size proves advantageous to both the user and to the programmer: The user has everything in one place; the programmer can group similar settings under the same tab while separating the dissimilar ones under other tabs. It is definitely user friendly to have all settings in one dialog box. However, such a setup also has disadvantages. If the tabbed dialog box has a Defaults or Apply button, for example, many users will be confused: They might wonder, "If I click on Defaults, will it affect the current tab only or all of them?" This is a real problem for the user. Consider, for example, a user who makes an important change in a tab, but can't remember it two weeks later (and it can't be seen). The user clicks on Defaults and his change is lost. When he returns to the application, he will wonder why something that worked fine before is totally different now.

Another potentially confusing aspect of this setup is that the Defaults button affects the visible tab only (the tab that is currently open). Assume, for example, that the user has hopelessly messed up his configurations. (This happens more often than developers might think.) The user opens the tabbed dialog box and clicks on Defaults and OK, but this action changes the visible tab only (perhaps to suboptimal, but usable, settings). All other tabs that were misconfigured earlier are still unchanged. It will take quite some time for the user to discover that he has to go through all tabs and click on every Defaults button to restore the standard configuration that he can use as a starting point for his customized settings.

Another possibility is to put every group of parameters in its own dialog box. Confusion is nearly impossible, but users have to deal with myriad dialog boxes in larger applications until they've customized everything to the way they want it. That's not very user friendly, but it is a little bit more secure.

I compromise by putting everything that at least loosely belongs together in one dialog box, and then I group each set of parameters within a frame. You can take a look at a similarly well-designed dialog box by opening KWrite ("Advanced Editor") and selecting the Defaults, Options, or Highlights items from the Options menu.

I place the groups TSP and optimization in one dialog box and its graphics in another one. At first, I focus on only the first dialog box. I promise up front that I'll make a substantial mistake. Only after that mistake is ironed out am I ready to turn my attention to other dialog boxes.

4.1 The Dialog Box, First Approach

First, install the next version of our program, ktsp-0.0.4.tgz, from the files on the New Riders website. Execute the optimizer KTsp and open the configurations dialog box by selecting Options, TSP Preferences. In the menu, an ellipsis (...) appears after the word *Preferences*. The ellipsis indicates that this menu entry opens a dialog box.

The dialog box that appears on your system might look quite different from what is shown here in Figure 4.1. If so, it's probably because your desktop style is set to Windows 95; my desktop style is set to Motif. A slider does looks very different in these two cases.

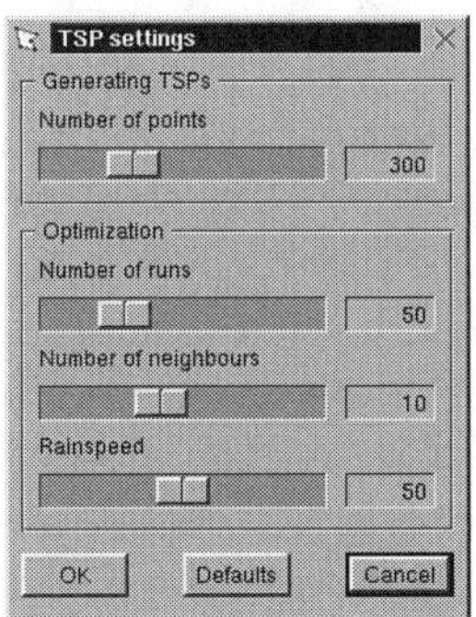

Figure 4.1 *The configuration dialog box.*

As planned, everything is placed in two framed blocks. The number of points is the only thing in the first block. Naturally, it affects a generated TSP only. If the user loads the TSP, the number of points will already be set. The lower limit for the number of points is set to 10. It doesn't make any sense to optimize smaller TSPs with the computer. The upper limit is at

1,000. The program has no problem with more points, but it will be hard to use the slider.

The second block contains the optimization parameters. The number of runs ranges between 1 and 200. You'll need a very fast computer for more than 200 runs. A lower number of runs is enough for testing purposes. With real optimizations, users are usually content with 50 to 100 runs. That's why 50 is a reasonable preset.

The number of neighbors that must be considered ranges from 3 to 20. Fewer than 3 won't lead to satisfying results. More than 20 is just unnecessary. After all, it's extremely unlikely that a connection from a Point A to a Point B that is farther away from A than 20 other points will lead to a well-optimized TSP. Actually, 10 is a reasonable preset number. The implementation of the optimization algorithm requests that the number of neighbors be at least one less than the number of points. In the dialog box, the two sliders are connected to each other so that this condition is always satisfied. Use 15 points and try to get more than 14 neighbors. It won't work. The same happens the other way around: You cannot get fewer than 21 points if you have 20 neighbors.

The rainfall speed can vary between 0 and 100. The preset number of 50 means that GDA lets it rain at the normal speed. 0 halves the amount of rainfall; 100 doubles it. The larger the amount of rainfall, the faster our algorithm (but worse for it).

The dialog box doesn't provide an input line where numbers can be directly inserted. (Users tend to write nonsense on those lines anyway, like their names when a program actually wants a number.) For integers, this works fine. KDE even provides a class that automatically takes care of that: KIntegerLine. Floating-point numbers are a nightmare, however, because of the different formats. In scientific format, there can be up to two negative signs, one for the mantissa and one for the exponent.

Only one negative sign is allowed in non-scientific format. You also have to pay attention to numbers where only half of the number is written and where a negative sign is at the end, which looks false but doesn't necessarily have to be. An input line that takes care of all floating-point number formats needs a real parser. If at all possible, I don't provide the user with an input line. This is my way of protecting them from crashing programs and myself from the work of catching all the faults.

Now for the source. First, as usual, the class declaration:

```
class TspDialog : public QDialog
  {
  Q_OBJECT

   public:
    TspDialog( int numberOfPoints,
```

```
            int numberOfPointsDefault,
            int numberOfRuns,
            int numberOfRunsDefault,
            int numberOfNeighbours,
            int numberOfNeighboursDefault,
            int rainspeedValue,
            int rainspeedValueDefault,
            QWidget *parent = 0,
            const char *name = 0 );
  ~TspDialog();

signals:
  void pointsChanged( int number );
  void runsChanged( int number );
  void neighboursChanged( int number );
  void rainspeedChanged( int number );

private slots:
  void slotOK();
  void slotDefaults();
  void slotCheckNeighbours( int number );
  void slotCheckPoints( int number );
  void slotCheckRuns( int number );
  void slotCheckRain( int number );

private:
  QGroupBox *tspGroup;
  QLabel *pointsText;
  QLabel *pointsNum;
  QSlider *pointsSlider;
  QGroupBox *optimizeGroup;
  QLabel *runsText;
  QLabel *runsNum;
  QSlider *runsSlider;
  QLabel *neighboursText;
  QLabel *neighboursNum;
  QSlider *neighboursSlider;
  QLabel *rainspeedText;
  QLabel *rainspeedNum;
  QSlider *rainspeedSlider;
  QPushButton *ok;
  QPushButton *defaults;
  QPushButton *cancel;

  int points;
  int pointsDefault;
  int runs;
  int runsDefault;
  int neighbours;
  int neighboursDefault;
  int rainspeed;
  int rainspeedDefault;
};
```

`TspDialog` is derived from QDialog. KDE doesn't provide its own basic dialog box class, KDialog, because Qt provides all the necessary functionality. The constructor of `TspDialog` looks like a real monster. Well, the dialog box can't know the current values used in the program. It needs to be informed about them. It could set the default values by itself. In my opinion, it will be simpler for changes in the program later if they're passed to the constructor. The parent widget is not so important because we create the dialog box on the stack. For the sake of consistency, however, I strongly suggest (read: plead) that you always specify a parent for widgets.

`TspDialog` informs the program with four slots about changed parameters when the user clicks on the OK button. Two of the private slots, `slotOk()` and `slotDefaults()`, are meant to react to the clicking of the OK and Defaults buttons. We don't need a slot for the Cancel button because the dialog box doesn't have to do anything else except close itself—and there's already a slot in QDialog for this event. The remaining four slots connect the sliders with their numeric displays and check the consistency of the number of points against the number of neighbors.

A large number of pointers to each widget follows here, and the internal variables where the constructor saves the parameters are also listed. A look at the definition of the constructor will hopefully explain how things work together:

```
// insert the first QGroupBox
tspGroup = new QGroupBox( i18n( "Generating TSPs" ),
                          this, "TSP Group");
CHECK_PTR( tspGroup );
tspGroup->setGeometry( 5, 5, 240, 78 );

// insert all widgets into the box
pointsText = new QLabel( i18n( "Number of points" ),
                         tspGroup, "Points Text" );
CHECK_PTR( pointsText );
pointsText->setGeometry( 10, 22, 160, 15 );

pointsSlider = new QSlider( 10, 1000, 1, points,
                            QSlider::Horizontal, tspGroup,
                           "Points Slider" );

CHECK_PTR( pointsSlider );
pointsSlider->setGeometry( 10, 45, 160, 20 );
connect( pointsSlider, SIGNAL( valueChanged( int ) ),
         this, SLOT( slotCheckPoints( int ) ) );

pointsNum = new QLabel( tspGroup, "Points Numeric" );
CHECK_PTR( pointsNum );
pointsNum->setNum( points );
pointsNum->setGeometry( 180, 45, 50, 20 );
pointsNum->setFrameStyle( QFrame::Panel | QFrame::Sunken );
pointsNum->setAlignment( AlignRight | AlignVCenter );
```

It's unnecessary to show the whole constructor, because things would repeat themselves over and over. We assume a 250-pixel-wide dialog box, for example. Consistent with that assumption, we insert a `QGroupBox` that is 240 pixels wide and 78 pixels high and whose upper-left corner is relative to the `QDialog` shifted 5 pixels to the right and to the bottom, which leaves a small border around the `QGroupBox`. We set the title in the QGroupBox and set the dialog box itself as the parent. It paints a frame within the QGroupBox and displays the title in the upper-left part of the frame.

It is important for the coordinates that `setGeometry()` sets to always refer to the parent widget. Because we create the following widgets with the `QGroupBox` as their parent, the coordinates correspond not to the dialog box, but to the `QGroupBox`. One after another, we insert a static QLabel that displays the meaning of the parameter, a QSlider over which we can change the value, and a dynamic QLabel that displays the currently valid value in the `QGroupBox`. To the constructor of the QSlider, we pass the minimum and maximum values as well as the increment that it will be moved to the left or to the right when a user clicks next to it (as opposed to a user dragging it). The starting value, the horizontal orientation, and the parent widget follow. Finally, we connect it to the private slot `slotCheckPoints()`, receiving the value QSlider emits. Every movement of the QSlider causes the slot to receive the value that corresponds to the new position of the QSlider. The slot then saves the value and tells the dynamic QLabel `pointsNum` to display it.

The last widget that we insert is the QLabel that's supposed to display the number of points in this `QGroupBox`. With `setFrameStyle()` and `setAlignment()`, we tell QLabel how is has to look and that the value has to be displayed aligned right and vertically centered.

The first group of parameters is inserted in the dialog box. The construction of the second `QGroupBox` functions the same way. The one important thing to remember is that the coordinates of the `QGroupBox` are relative to the dialog box, and that the coordinates of the inserted widgets refer to the `QGroupBox`. At the end of the constructor, we give the dialog box a fixed size and use the `methodsetCaption()` to create a relevant title:

```
setFixedSize( 250, 315 );
setCaption( i18n( "TSP settings" ) );
```

Only the OK, Defaults, and Cancel buttons are missing:

```
ok = new QPushButton( i18n( "OK" ), this, "TSP OK" );
CHECK_PTR( ok );
ok->setGeometry( 5, 280, 60, 25 );
connect( ok, SIGNAL( clicked() ), this, SLOT( slotOK() ) );
ok->setDefault( true );
defaults = new QPushButton( i18n( "Defaults" ), this,
                            "TSP Defaults);
```

```
CHECK_PTR( defaults );
defaults->setGeometry( 95, 280, 60, 25 );
connect( defaults, SIGNAL( clicked() ), this,
         SLOT( slotDefaults() ) );

cancel = new QPushButton( i18n( "Cancel" ), this,
                          "TSP Cancel" );

CHECK_PTR( cancel );
cancel->setGeometry( 185, 280, 60, 25 );
connect( cancel, SIGNAL( clicked() ), this, SLOT( reject() ) );
```

The OK and the Defaults buttons are connected to their own slots, but the Cancel button is connected to the `reject()` slot, which is already built in to QDialog.

With `setDefault()`, we specify the OK button as the default button (not to be confused with our own Defaults button). As a result, the Return key will press the OK button. Every dialog box should specify the button that can do the least damage as the default button to prevent users from unwillingly damaging the program. In this case, the OK button applies the changes in the program and, therefore, is the natural candidate for the default button.

Okay, we have created the dialog box. Now as one example of the four slots that receive the values of the slider, we'll take a look at `slotCheckPoints()`:

```
void TspDialog::slotCheckPoints( int number )
  {
  if ( number <= neighbours )
    {
    // points must be greater than neighbours
    // we just reset QSlider to the old value and don't
    // do anything else
    pointsSlider->setValue( points );
    }
  else
    {
    points = number;
    pointsNum->setNum( points );
    }
  }
```

The first branch of the *if* statement prevents the number of points from being smaller or equal to the number of the neighbors. It's impossible to leave the range of values; the corresponding slider won't even send those values.

The second branch saves the value and calls `setNum()` of the corresponding QLabel, which then displays the new value. The other three slots function just the same way. Let's take a look at the `slotDefaults()` slot, which is called when the Defaults button has been clicked:

```
void TspDialog::slotDefaults()
  {
  points = pointsDefault;
  pointsSlider->setValue( points );

  runs = runsDefault;
  runsSlider->setValue( runs );

  neighbours = neighboursDefault;
  neighboursSlider->setValue( neighbours );

  rainspeed = rainspeedDefault;
  rainspeedSlider->setValue( rainspeed );
  }
```

The slot first sets the Default value as the current one, and then calls `setValue()` of the corresponding slider for all four values. At that point, the QSlider sends its signal `valueChanged()` and our previously discussed four slots take care of adjusting the corresponding dynamic QLabel. That's why we don't have to bother with them. The slot `slotOK()` is the last one that we have to talk about:

```
void TspDialog::slotOK()
  {
  emit pointsChanged( points );
  emit runsChanged( runs );
  emit neighboursChanged( neighbours );
  emit rainspeedChanged( rainspeed );
  accept();
  }
```

It just sends the signals for the four values, and then calls the slot `accept()` of QDialog, which closes the dialog box.[1] We declared all of our widgets either directly or indirectly over a `QGroupBox` as children of the dialog box. That's why we don't have bother with them when the dialog box is closed. When the dialog box gets deleted, our widgets' memory will be freed.

That's all we need to discuss about the inner life of our `TspDialog`. It looks pretty good, doesn't it? It even works. Try it. The changed values really affect the program. The user can create differently sized TSPs and influence the optimization. In short, it works; nevertheless, the dialog box has a fundamental fault.

1 *... and calls the slot. Yes, it's really possible. Because a slot is an ordinary function, it can be called. This is very practical. We can connect a slot to a signal; we can also connect our own slot to a signal, take care of some things in our slot, and then directly call it.*

Please change the font as well as the font size with the help of the KDE Control Center or in KPanel by selecting K, Settings, Desktop, Fonts. Choose the Lucida font and 16 as the font size. Now open the dialog box again. Oh my, it doesn't look that good anymore! I'm not talking about the font itself. It could be that the corresponding font size is not installed on your system. Okay, in this case, it will look bad. I'm talking about the dialog box itself. The word *Defaults* doesn't fit on the button anymore, and overall the dialog box just doesn't seem balanced.

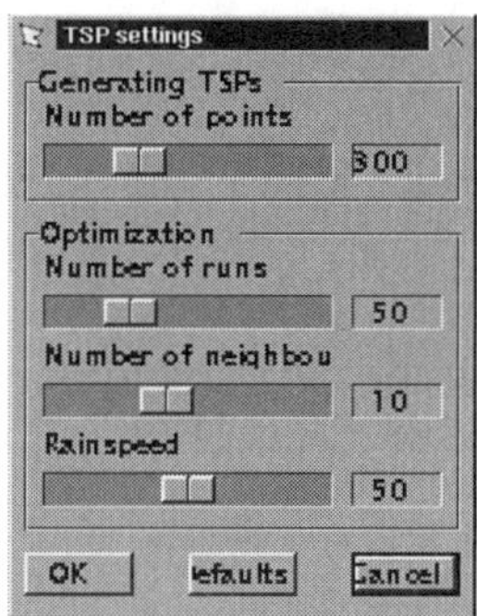

Figure 4.2 *The consequences of fixed widget sizes.*

We just statically defined the sizes of all widgets! Naturally, changes to font type or size will lead to problems, but it gets worse. So far, there're no translations for KTsp. Let's assume that a Finnish translation already exists and someone uses KDE in Finnish (with all those very long Finnish words). The user probably won't be able to read anything. After all, we prepared all texts with `i18n()` for the translation; we never considered that words have different lengths in different languages.

So now what? Is there a way out?

4.2 Layouts

I've got good and bad news. First the good news: Yes, rescue is possible. We can develop dialog boxes so that they can adapt to different font sizes and different languages. Now the bad news: It's hard work. An easy way doesn't exist (yet). This time KDE won't do the work for us. We have to take care of it by ourselves.

4.2.1 QLayout

The Trolls ship their libraries with layout managers based on QLayout. The following discussion is restricted to the two most important managers (in my mind)—QVBoxLayout and QHBoxLayout—and covers almost all of the various situations.

So far, I have managed to immediately use the new things that we learn about KDE and Qt in our example program, KTsp. It's not possible with the layout management, however. If we looked directly at the source of `TspDialog`, the principles of the layout managers and how they are used would not become immediately clear. It's a somewhat complicated subject whose explanation takes a little more time. Although the content is pretty dry and hard to digest, it is definitely worth hanging in there and reading everything about this theme. In the end, you'll be rewarded with the ability to write dialog boxes and even whole programs that are totally independent of the language, font type, and font size, because they won't make any assumptions about the size of any widgets.

What Are Layout Managers?

This section uses `QHBoxLayout` as an example of a layout manager. This type of layout lines up an unlimited number of widgets in a horizontal row.

Figure 4.3 *Horizontal layout management with three buttons.*

The size of the widgets is equally preset, and they get compressed or stretched in a such a way that they horizontally fill the provided space. The width of the parent widget (in our case, the dialog box) defines the amount of provided space. Figure 4.3 shows such a dialog box, which is made of three `QPushButtons`. The dialog box can be magnified arbitrarily or reduced to a minimal size, as desired. The buttons grow or shrink with the dialog box created by the following class declaration and definition:

```
class MyDialog : public QDialog
  {
  public:
    MyDialog();
  };

MyDialog::MyDialog()
  {
  QHBoxLayout *layout = new QHBoxLayout( this );
  CHECK_PTR( layout );

  QPushButton *button;
  QString s;
```

```
  for ( int i = 1; i < 4; i++ )
    {
    s.sprintf( "Button %d", i );
    button = new QPushButton( s, this );
    CHECK_PTR( button );
    button->setMinimumSize( button->sizeHint() );
    layout->addWidget( button );
    }
  layout->activate();
  }
```

The declaration is trivial. In the definition of the constructor, we provide a `QHBoxLayout` first whose parent widget is the dialog box itself and a pointer to a `QPushButton`. A button is created in every run of the loop. Just like every QWidget, every `QPushButton` has a member function `sizeHint()`, which points out an appropriate size of the button. We set this value as the minimal size of the button (which the button cannot fall short of). With `layout->addWidget()`, we insert the buttons one after the other in the layout. As we use a `QHBoxLayout`, the widgets will be inserted from left to right.

Finally, we activate the Layout Mechanism with `layout->activate()`. From this moment on, the three buttons will always completely fill the dialog box, no matter how much it grows or shrinks—with the exception that the minimal size of the buttons, which we've set in the loop, determine the minimal size of the dialog box.

Take a closer look at Figure 4.3. In that figure, you'll see that the statement is meant literally. The buttons really fill the whole dialog box. The small frame around it doesn't belong to the dialog box; it is added to every window by the Windows Manager. This filling of the space isn't necessarily what the programmer wants to have. As a rule, we want a little border there. Also, the widgets should not lie directly beside each other; they should have a little space in between them.

Figure 4.4 *Layout with three buttons and some space between them.*

`QHBoxLayout` provides the method `addSpacing()`, enabling us to add spaces between widgets. Figure 4.4 shows the result that was affected by making just a small change in the constructor:

```
MyDialog::MyDialog()
  {
  QHBoxLayout *layout = new QHBoxLayout( this );
  CHECK_PTR( layout );

  QPushButton *button;
```

```
QString s;

layout->addSpacing( 10 );
for ( int i = 1; i < 4; i++ )
  {
  s.sprintf( "Button %d", i );
  button = new QPushButton( s, this );
  CHECK_PTR( button );
  button->setMinimumSize( button->sizeHint() );
  layout->addWidget( button );
  if ( i < 3 ) layout->addSpacing( 15 );
  }
layout->addSpacing( 10 );
layout->activate();
}
```

First, we use `addSpacing()` to add a 10-pixel space in front of the *for* loop. That space will serve as the left border. The *for* loop itself uses `addSpacing()` to create a 15-pixel space between the buttons and, after the loop, a 10-pixel space for the right border. The result already looks better.

Figure 4.5 *Layout with different sized buttons.*

We still can't be satisfied with it. The three widgets are still the same size; this might not be good enough to meet the requirements of a real dialog box.

Several methods can help us realize different sized buttons. Instead of `setMinimumSize()`, we can use the member function `setFixedSize()`, for example, with one of the widgets. This will ensure that the widget won't take part in the growing and shrinking of the dialog box. Figure 4.5 shows such a dialog box. I modified the text on the buttons in such a way that their smallest width is smaller than in the last example so that the difference between them would be more prominent. The changes in the source look like this:

```
MyDialog::MyDialog()
  {
  QHBoxLayout *layout = new QHBoxLayout( this );
  CHECK_PTR( layout );

  QPushButton *button;
  QString s;

  layout->addSpacing( 10 );
  for ( int i = 1; i < 3; i++ )
    {
```

```
    s.sprintf( "B %d", i );
    button = new QPushButton( s, this );
    CHECK_PTR( button );
    button->setMinimumSize( button->sizeHint() );
    layout->addWidget( button );
    layout->addSpacing( 15 );
    }
  button = new QPushButton( "B 3", this );
  CHECK_PTR( button );
  button->setFixedSize( button->sizeHint() );
  layout->addWidget( button );
  layout->addSpacing( 10 );
  layout->activate();
  }
```

This time I left the third button out of the loop, because we have to treat it in a different way from the others. We use `setFixedSize()` to set its size to exactly the one we get from `sizeHint()`. We have to be aware that within the layout at least one element can always change its size. It doesn't need to be a widget. Spaces can change their sizes, too. We use the QHBoxLayout method `addStretch()`, which inserts something like a rubber band that can be stretched (and contracted as well) between the widgets. Figure 4.6 shows the result.

Figure 4.6 *Layout with three buttons and "rubber bands."*

The changes in the source are as follows:

```
  layout->addSpacing( 10 );

  for ( int i = 1; i < 3; i++ )
    {
    s.sprintf( "B %d", i );
    button = new QPushButton( s, this );
    CHECK_PTR( button );
    button->setFixedSize( button->sizeHint() );
    layout->addWidget( button );
    layout->addSpacing( 15 );
    layout->addStretch();
    }

  button = new QPushButton( "B 3", this );
  CHECK_PTR( button );
  button->setMinimumSize( button->sizeHint() );
  layout->addWidget( button );
  layout->addSpacing( 10 );
  layout->activate();
```

I'll only show the relevant parts from now on; you surely know the rest by heart now. This time both of the first buttons in the loop get a fixed size, and the third one outside the loop gets the minimal size. In the loop, we add a fixed size of 15 pixels as space that must be kept. Additionally, we use `addStretch()` to insert the "rubber band."

Figure 4.7 *Layout with stretch factors.*

The remaining possible way to influence the size proportions of the widgets within the layout is to let them grow and shrink at different speeds. There's no known function for this. We just add an additional "stretch factor" in `addWidget()`. They are integers whose absolute values don't matter. Only the ratios between the stretch factors are important. If we insert widget A with a factor of 1 and widget B with a factor of 2 into a layout, B will grow or shrink twice as fast as A. A factor 0 means that there's no change to the size of the widget.

Using stretch factors together with `addStretch()` and `setFixedSize()` doesn't make much sense. The results are totally unexpected.[2] If you use the stretch factor, set only the minimal sizes of the widgets and don't use `addStretch()`. If you use stretch factors, you should specify them for every widget in the layout.

It works with other ways, too; but as a rule, not as it is expected. A corresponding dialog box can be seen in Figure 4.7. The changes in the source have a greater extent this time:

```
layout->addSpacing( 10 );

button = new QPushButton( "B 1", this );
CHECK_PTR( button );
button->setMinimumSize( button->sizeHint() );
layout->addWidget( button, 1 );
layout->addSpacing( 15 );

button = new QPushButton( "B 2", this );
CHECK_PTR( button );
button->setMinimumSize( button->sizeHint() );
layout->addWidget( button, 2 );
layout->addSpacing( 15 );
```

[2] *You can achieve interesting "special effects" by using combinations of stretch factors and* `setFixedSize()`, *but the results won't look as expected in most of the cases (and it will take a lot of testing before everything works). It's better to just leave it alone.*

```
button = new QPushButton( "B 3", this );
CHECK_PTR( button );
button->setMinimumSize( button->sizeHint() );
layout->addWidget( button, 0 );

layout->addSpacing( 10 );
layout->activate();
```

We have given up the *for* loop because we treat every button differently now anyway. You can already see why layouts result in a lot of source. Sure, Copy and Paste or a programmable editor can save a lot of work. Still, dialog boxes with layout managers certainly require a lot more work than dialog boxes without managers—although the annoying position and size calculations are omitted.

Now it's time to consider the source. We insert 10 pixels at the left and right border with `addSpacing()`, and we insert 15 pixels between the buttons. So far so good. All `addStretch()` calls have been eliminated. The minimal size of all buttons is set with `setMinimumSize()`. While inserting them into the layout, button 1 gets a stretch factor of 1, button 2 gets a stretch factor of 2, and button 3 gets a stretch factor of 0. Therefore, button 2 grows or shrinks faster than button 1, but the size of button 3 doesn't change.

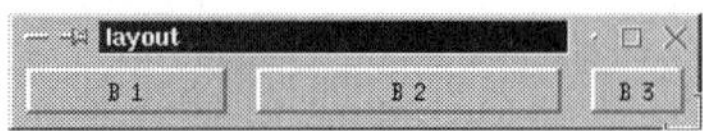

Figure 4.8 *A horizontal layout with a border around it.*

One unsatisfying property of the dialog box remains. Take a look at Figure 4.7. On the left and the right of our button, a border appears just like we wanted it to. However, the buttons still fill the whole vertical space of the dialog box. We want a border all around it for aesthetic reasons. Now, `QHBoxLayout` can insert things in the horizontal direction only. It's not responsible for the vertical direction. Now what? Fortunately, the constructor of the layout enables us to specify the size of a frame that is left free around the layout. Figure 4.8 shows the result. The changes in the source are minimal:

```
MyDialog::MyDialog()
  {
  QHBoxLayout *hlayout = new QHBoxLayout( this, 5 );
  CHECK_PTR( hlayout );

  QPushButton *button;
  button = new QPushButton( "B 1", this );
  CHECK_PTR( button );
```

```
button->setMinimumSize( button->sizeHint() );
hlayout->addWidget( button, 1 );
hlayout->addSpacing( 15 );

// source for adding two other buttons deleted
hlayout->activate();
}
```

This time we create the `QHBoxLayout` with two parameters in the constructor: The first one is just like we're used to, a pointer to the dialog box; the second one specifies how big the free border around the layout is supposed to be. We can leave out the call of `addSpacing()` at the beginning and at the end because we automatically get the border—and this time, we get it above and below the layout as well.

This takes us to the end of a simple `QHBoxLayout`. What's left to say is that `QVBoxLayout` provides the same functionality for vertical rows of widgets. Widgets are inserted from top to bottom in `QVBoxLayouts`.

More Complex Layouts

Dialog boxes normally don't consist of just a row of three buttons. Usually they consist of a couple of widgets that display something, and some that let the user change things, and of buttons that transfer the changes to the program or cancel the changes. Figure 4.9 shows a simple example of such a dialog box.

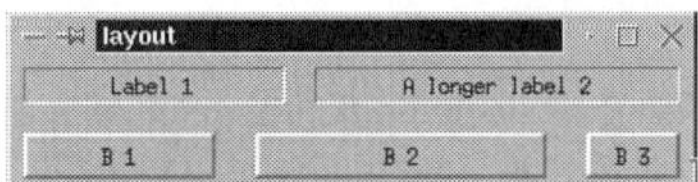

Figure 4.9 *Dialog boxes with buttons and labels.*

The source of this dialog box is as follows:

```
MyDialog::MyDialog()
  {
  QVBoxLayout *vlayout = new QVBoxLayout( this, 5 );
  CHECK_PTR( vlayout );

  QHBoxLayout *hlayout1 = new QHBoxLayout();
  CHECK_PTR( hlayout1 );

  QHBoxLayout *hlayout2 = new QHBoxLayout();
  CHECK_PTR( hlayout2 );

  vlayout->addLayout( hlayout1 );
  vlayout->addSpacing( 10 );
  vlayout->addLayout( hlayout2 );
```

```
QLabel *label = new QLabel( "Label 1", this );
CHECK_PTR( label );
label->adjustSize();
label->setMinimumSize( label->width(),
              label->height() + 6 );
label->setFrameStyle( QFrame::Panel | QFrame::Sunken );
label->setAlignment( AlignCenter );
hlayout1->addWidget( label );
hlayout1->addSpacing( 10 );

label = new QLabel( "A longer label 2", this );
CHECK_PTR( label );
label->adjustSize();
label->setMinimumSize( label->width(),
              label->height() + 6 );
label->setFrameStyle( QFrame::Panel | QFrame::Sunken );
label->setAlignment( AlignCenter );
hlayout1->addWidget( label );

QPushButton *button = new QPushButton( "B 1", this );
CHECK_PTR( button );
button->setMinimumSize( button->sizeHint() );
hlayout2->addWidget( button, 1 );
hlayout2->addSpacing( 15 );

button = new QPushButton( "B 2", this );
CHECK_PTR( button );
button->setMinimumSize( button->sizeHint() );
hlayout2->addWidget( button, 2 );
hlayout2->addSpacing( 15 );

button = new QPushButton( "B 3", this );
CHECK_PTR( button );
button->setMinimumSize( button->sizeHint() );
hlayout2->addWidget( button, 0 );

vlayout->activate();
}
```

This time we create a `QVBoxLayout` with the dialog box as the parent and a 5-pixel wide border. Next, we create two other layouts of the type `QHBoxLayout` without a widget as the parent. This is important. Layouts can be inserted in other layouts, too, not just widgets; but they are not allowed to have a parent. The top-level layout that has a parent manages the geometry of the whole widget. All the others that have been inserted in the top one with `addLayout()` manage parts of the space the widget provides.

After we've created three layouts, we insert the two horizontal ones with `addLayout()` in the vertical. We insert a 10-pixel space between them. Parentless layouts have to be inserted in another layout before their member functions can be called. The QLabels are inserted, just like we're used to, in the first horizontal layout; the buttons go into the second one. At the end, we activate the top-level layout that has the dialog box as its parent with `activate()`. Only the top-level one is being activated! Child layouts start their layout management at the time the parent layout gets activated.

Two remarks about the QLabels are relevant here. We display them sunken so that the whole label is visible. The default settings make it invisible so that only the text is visible; we wouldn't have an impression about how big the label actually is. The minimal size is set in a somewhat strange way. It's because `sizeHint()` of a QLabel returns the exact height of the font. That's okay for the default settings where the label itself isn't visible, but doesn't look very good with the sunken style that we've chosen. The method `adjustSize()` is equivalent to `label->setSize( label->sizeHint() )`. The label will have the size that `sizeHint()` returns. After that, we add 6 pixels to the height and set the whole thing as the minimum size.

Complicated Layouts

As pointed out earlier, I usually want frames (`QGroupBox`) around parts of my dialog box that belong together. The best dialog boxes of KDE are built like this, but it creates a new problem. `QGroupBox` is no empty widget. It draws a frame within itself and a title in the frame. However, Qt's layout managers pay attention only to the pure geometry of the widget and not to what has been drawn within the widget.

The other question is this: Because `QGroupBox` is a widget that contains other widgets (which the programmer inserts), how can we insert something like that in a layout? Layouts contain layouts and/or widgets. If we insert a `QGroupBox` in a layout, who will manage the layout of the widgets within?

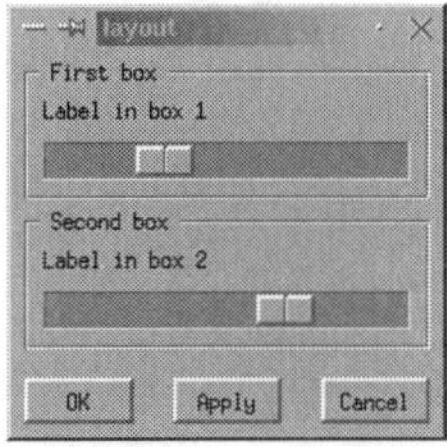

Figure 4.10 *Layout management of a complicated dialog box.*

Qt's online Help states that more than one layout with a parent widget will confuse the layout management. Although this statement is correct, it often leads developers to the false assumption that there can't be more than one layout with a parent in one class. That is wrong!

Multiple layouts with the same parent are not allowed. In the case of the QGroupBox, we don't have any choice but to specify the QGroupBox as the parent of a layout that manages the geometry of the widgets within the QGroupBox. This means that we need a top-level layout with a parent for the dialog box itself as well as one for every QGroupBox that we insert in the dialog box. Figure 4.10 shows the results of our efforts. Because this dialog box is a little bit more complicated than the previous ones, the constructor is longer as well:

```
MyDialog::MyDialog()
  {
  QGroupBox *box1 = new QGroupBox( "First box", this,
                                   "First QGroupBox");
  CHECK_PTR( box1 );

  QGroupBox *box2 = new QGroupBox( "Second box", this,
                                    "Second QGroupBox");
  CHECK_PTR( box2 );

  QVBoxLayout *vlayout = new QVBoxLayout( this, 5 );
  CHECK_PTR( vlayout );

  QHBoxLayout *hlayout = new QHBoxLayout();

  QVBoxLayout *box1layout = new QVBoxLayout( box1, 10 );
  CHECK_PTR( box1layout );

  QVBoxLayout *box2layout = new QVBoxLayout( box2, 10 );
  CHECK_PTR( box2layout );

  vlayout->addWidget( box1 );
  vlayout->addWidget( box2 );
  vlayout->addSpacing( 10 );
  vlayout->addLayout( hlayout );

  box1layout->addSpacing( 10 );

  QLabel *label = new QLabel( "Label in box 1", box1 );
  CHECK_PTR( label );
  label->setMinimumSize( label->sizeHint() );
  box1layout->addWidget( label );

  QSlider *slider = new QSlider( 1, 100, 1, 30,
                                 QSlider::Horizontal, box1,
                                 "Box1 Slider" );

  CHECK_PTR( slider );
  slider->setMinimumSize( 100, 20 );
  box1layout->addWidget( slider );

  box2layout->addSpacing( 10 );
```

```
label = new QLabel( "Label in box 2", box2 );
CHECK_PTR( label );
label->setMinimumSize( label->sizeHint() );
box2layout->addWidget( label );

slider = new QSlider( 1, 100, 1, 70,
                      QSlider::Horizontal, box2,
                      "Box2 Slider" );
slider->setMinimumSize( 100, 20 );
box2layout->addWidget( slider );

QPushButton *button1 = new QPushButton( "OK", this );
CHECK_PTR( button1 );
button1->setMinimumSize( button1->sizeHint() );
hlayout->addWidget( button1 );
hlayout->addSpacing( 15 );
hlayout->addStretch();

QPushButton *button2 = new QPushButton( "Apply", this );
CHECK_PTR( button2 );
button2->setMinimumSize( button2->sizeHint() );
hlayout->addWidget( button2 );
hlayout->addSpacing( 15 );
hlayout->addStretch();

QPushButton *button3 = new QPushButton( "Cancel", this );
CHECK_PTR( button3 );
button3->setMinimumSize( button3->sizeHint() );
hlayout->addWidget( button3 );

QSize s = button1->sizeHint();
if ( button2->sizeHint().width() > s.width() )
                s.setWidth( button2->sizeHint().width() );
if ( button3->sizeHint().width() > s.width() )
                s.setWidth( button3->sizeHint().width() );
s.setWidth( s.width() - 10 );
button1->setFixedSize( s );
button2->setFixedSize( s );
button3->setFixedSize( s );

box1layout->activate();
box2layout->activate();
vlayout->activate();

resize( 0, 0 );
vlayout->freeze();
}
```

We create all necessary QGroupBoxes and layouts right at the beginning to arrange the constructor in a more understandable way. We create the layout that manages the whole dialog box with a 5-pixel-wide border and the dialog box as parent. Either of the two layouts that manage the two QGroupBoxes gets a border of 10 pixels and the appropriate QGroupBox as parent. This way, we end up with three top-level layouts with parents. The important part is that they are children of different parents. All three of them are vertical layouts. Additionally, we create a horizontal layout for the buttons at the bottom of the dialog box. This one has no parent because it will be inserted in the main layout.

The next step is to build the top level of the dialog box. For this, we insert each `QGroupBox` with `addWidget()` into the main layout. Afterwards, `addSpacing()` inserts a space of 10 pixels to separate the buttons from the rest of the dialog box a bit. Finally, `addLayout()` inserts the horizontal layout that will contain the buttons.

Now we'll deal with the first `QGroupBox`. The box layout (as I will call the layout that manages the `QGroupBox` from now on) has a border when created to protect its frame from being overlapped by the widgets we'll insert. This border won't be wide enough at the top because of the title written in the frame. Therefore, with `addSpacing()`, we insert a bit more space.

Within the box, we create two widgets—a `QLabel` and a `Qslider`—with the box as parent and insert them into the box layout. This doesn't present any surprise any more. The parameters we pass to the constructor of the `QSlider` are the minimum value (represented by the leftmost position of the slider), the maximum value for the rightmost position, the increment (the value will be increased or decreased if the user clicks to the right or left side of the little knob), and the starting value. The horizontal orientation, the parent widget, the `Qt` internal name we have already talked about several times. The method `sizeHint()` doesn't make much sense with a slider. What would be the smallest reasonable size of a slider? It depends on how large we want it to be! Accordingly, we set its minimum size directly in pixels. We construct the second box in a similar way.

Finally, we create the three buttons and insert them into the horizontal layout. The only interesting thing about this is the way their sizes are determined. This time, each button has another text written on itself; accordingly, `sizeHint()` returns a different width for each button. That doesn't look good. All buttons should be the same size; the width of each must be determined by the longest word. We find out this biggest width with the following lines.

Because this dialog box contains three top-level layouts (those with parents), we have to start layout management explicitly with `activate()` for all of them. If we forget about it, we'll get very strange results. The last two lines of the constructor are something new. We shrink the dialog box we have just created to a point with `resize( 0, 0 )`. Naturally, the layout management won't allow this and instead resizes it to the next larger size, which of course is the minimum size in which the dialog box can be displayed.

The last line calls the method `freeze()` of the top-level layout. This method terminates all layout management and makes the size of the dialog box fixed. If we won't let the user change the size, why all the effort with this many layouts? Three reasons force us to do this: different fonts, different font sizes, and different languages. Layout management always creates the dialog box at the correct size.

Actually, we should have called `freeze()` for each of the three top-level layouts. If the dialog box itself cannot change its size, however, its elements can't do it either.

5

KTsp Forgets Everything!

Not everything happening in KDE is in the GUI. Let's leave the screen for a moment and take care of this annoying property of our program, KTsp. We've now configured our program just as we want it: Points are medium-sized squares connected through thick red dotted lines, and everything is lost after leaving the program. The next time we start the program, the preset settings with small blue dots and red lines are restored. KTsp forgets everything between the executions. That's not what users have in mind when they think about a comfortable piece of software. In this chapter, we want to give KTsp a long-term memory.

5.1 The Directory .kde in the Home Directory

In the home directory of every user, KDE creates a hidden directory called `.kde`. It contains a lot of information about the individual programs in it. The directory tree of `$HOME/.kde` normally looks like that shown in Figure 5.1. Under `$HOME/.kde/share/apps`, you can see another bunch of directories with the names of popular KDE programs. That's where applications can save their application-specific files. The other interesting directory is `$HOME/.kde/share/config`. All the configuration files of the programs that have been started at least once are in it, with the name of the program and *rc* (for "resources") appended to the name. It would be "ktsprc" for our program; and actually there's really a file in it, but it's empty because we haven't saved the configuration yet.

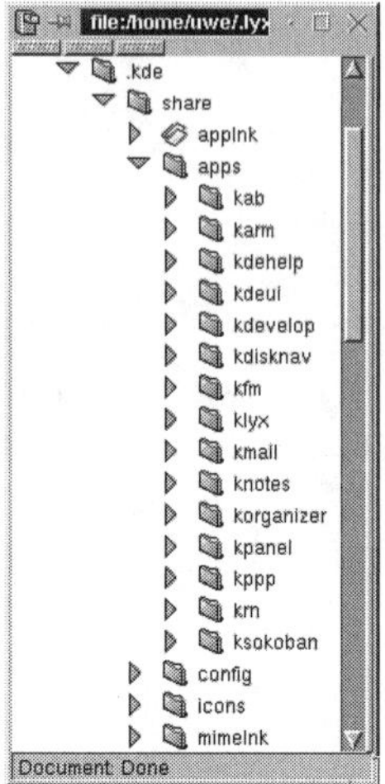

Figure 5.1 *The directory tree under* `$(HOME)/.kde`.

5.2 KConfig

The configuration files are pure ASCII files and are readable by humans just like any text editor. I don't want to encourage you to change this file by hand at all. It's the opposite: Hands away from it! If something goes wrong and the files are corrupt, it is really practical and useful that the user—or if not you, then probably the system administrator—can repair the configuration.[1] All configuration files have the following structure:

```
# KDE Config File
[Group name]
Parameter name=value
```

The first line characterizes the file as a configuration file. Names of groups of parameters appear in the rectangular brackets. Such names might include Colours, Appearance, Fonts, or any other name of a corresponding group of program-important parameters. Within every group, the corresponding parameters are listed. Every line contains the parameter name, an equal sign, and on the right side of the equal sign (the "equals" side), the value that has to be set. The value could be a string, such as a number. In an email program, the configuration file could contain the following section:

[1] *That's why KDE has chosen this form for configuration files. It takes a little bit longer to read and evaluate them than is the case with binary files, but they can be repaired rather easily.*

```
[Identity]
Address=uwe@kde.org
Reply-To Address=uwe@kde.org
Name=Uwe Thiem
Organisation=Uncle Uwe2
Signature=/home/uwe/.signature
```

Everything to the right of the equal sign is given to the program as a configuration parameter. Naturally, it would be senseless to leave it to the program to have its parser for the configuration file. If we did so, every programmer would have his own structure for the files, and such a situation would create unnecessary work for the programmer. That's why KDE provides the class KConfig, which pretty much takes care of everything for us.

As programmers, we don't have to worry about creating an instance of the class (KApplication takes care of that for us), just like we don't have to bother with loading or saving the file or the evaluation of the content. All we have to do is to specify the items that we want and the corresponding values.

Please install ktsp-0.0.6.tgz (from the New Riders website) on your system so that we can take a look at the method `KTsp::saveConfig()`:

```
void KTsp::saveConfig()
{
  KConfig *config = kapp->getConfig();
  config->setGroup( "Graphic" );
  config->writeEntry( "PointShape", _pointsShape );
  config->writeEntry( "PointColour", _pointsColour );
  config->writeEntry( "PointSize", _pointsSize );
  config->writeEntry( "LineStyle", _linesStyle );
  config->writeEntry( "LineColour", _linesColour );
  config->writeEntry( "LineWidth", _linesWidth );

  config->setGroup( "Optimization" );
  config->writeEntry( "Points", tsp->numberOfPoints() );
  config->writeEntry( "Neighbours", tsp->numberOfNeighbours() );
  config->writeEntry( "Runs", _runs );
  config->writeEntry( "Rainspeed", tsp->confFactor() );
  }
```

KApplication is kind enough to provide us with a pointer to the global instance of KConfig. We assign a local pointer so that we can access it more easily. With `setGroup()`, we set the name of the corresponding group of parameters (Graphic, in this case). With `writeEntry()`, we write the current

[2] *In many Namibian cultures (actually, in African cultures in general), uncle has a special meaning. The uncle is the eldest brother of the mother. His role corresponds to a great extent, but not completely, to the role of the father in European cultures. What does this have to do with KDE? In short: nothing.*

values in the configurations; the first parameter of the method is the name, and the second one is the value. This method is overloaded multiple times. The second function parameter can be a string or a number of any kind. We repeat the same for the optimization parameters. KConfig looks after the rest.

Let's turn toward an interesting question now: Where in our program should we call this method? The obvious approach would be in the destructor of the class KTsp, but we have to think about KApplication, QApplication, and KTMainWindow (which are in the background of our application). We don't know the time when the objects get deleted and the corresponding destructor gets called. It could be that the instance of KConfig doesn't even exist anymore at the time `KTsp::~KTsp()` gets called. Such a situation will lead to a program crash at the termination.

We have to think about a better version. `KTsp::slotQuit()` is the next-best candidate. It is called when the user clicks on File, Quit or on the Quit button in the toolbar, or if Ctrl+Q is pressed. The call is really in there:

```
void KTsp::slotQuit()
  {
  // Stop all calculations, save configuration and quit.
  tsp->stop();
  saveConfig();
  kapp->quit();
  }
```

Now we've taken care of almost all possibilities. A click on the X in the title bar of the window closes it. If it is the last window of the application, KTMainWindow terminates the program without the slot above getting called. Naturally, we want to include this case so that KTsp saves its configuration. The virtual function `queryClose()` of KTMW comes to our rescue. We have already used this function before, to stop the optimization before the data structures are destroyed at the termination of the program:

```
bool KTsp::queryClose()
  {
  tsp->stop();
  saveConfig();
  return true;
  }
```

We've already overwritten this virtual method. The only thing left to do is to call `saveConfig()` in it. Now we have really covered all possibilities regarding how the program can terminate. If we also want to take care of abnormal terminations (`Segfaults,...`), we would have to install signal handlers (not Qt signals, but UNIX signals).

If you have taken a close look at `ktmainwindow.h`, you have probably noticed that it contains the virtual method `queryExit()` as well as `queryClose()`. What's the difference? Well, `queryClose()` is called when the user closes a window derived from KTMW; KTMW terminates the application if the last window of KTMW is being closed. When closing the last window, `queryClose()` is called, and so is `queryExit()`. You can use this method to do some cleaning up that should be done after the last window is closed. If `queryClose()` returns false, the window won't be able to be close (who knows what that's good for?). If `queryExit()` returns false, all windows will be closed, but the program itself will still run. Avoid creating this situation in the source; otherwise, you could end up with a program that the user won't be able to control after it is closed.

The configuration file `ktsprc` looks like this:

```
# KDE Config File
[Optimization]
Points=489
Runs=20
Neighbours=12
Rainspeed=40
[Graphic]
LineColour=0
LineWidth=0
PointShape=0
LineStyle=0
PointSize=1
PointColour=2
```

Of course, the concrete values can differ from yours. After KTsp has saved its configuration on the hard disk, we must enable it to read it at the start. The corresponding code can be found in `KTsp::readConfig()`:

```
void KTsp::readConfig()
  {
  KConfig *config = kapp->getConfig();
  config->setGroup( "Graphic" );
  _pointsShape = config->readNumEntry( "PointShape",
                                      GraphicDialog::Circle );
  _pointsColour = config->readNumEntry( "PointColour",
                                       GraphicDialog::Blue );
  _pointsSize = config->readNumEntry( "PointSize",
                                     GraphicDialog::Small );
  _linesStyle = config->readNumEntry( "LineStyle",
                                     GraphicDialog::Solid );
  _linesColour = config->readNumEntry( "LineColour",
                                      GraphicDialog::Red );
  _linesWidth = config->readNumEntry( "LineWidth",
                                     GraphicDialog::Small );
  config->setGroup( "Optimization" );
  tsp->setNumberOfPoints( config->readNumEntry( "Points", 300 ) );
  tsp->setNumberOfNeighbours( config->readNumEntry(
                                   "Neighbours", 10 ) );
  tsp->setConfFactor( config->readNumEntry( "Rainspeed", 50 ) );
  _runs = config->readNumEntry( "Runs", 50 );
  }
```

First, we let KApplication give us a pointer to the global instance KConfig. Then, we assign it to a local pointer so that we can access it more easily. Finally, we set the group to `"Graphic"`. Because overloaded functions aren't allowed to have a different return type only, KConfig provides a bunch of reading functions: `readEntry()` reads a string; `readNumEntry()` does the same as for an integer. The other methods can be found in `kconfig.h`; the names should be clear.

All reading functions of KConfig have two parameters. The first one is a string with the name of the parameter. The second one is a default value, which will be returned by the method if the name of the parameter isn't found in the configuration file.[3] The code in `readConfig()` is self-explanatory: We read all the parameters one after the other and assign them to the corresponding variables in the program. Again, the question arises: Where is `readConfig()` supposed to be called? The answer is really easy in this case: at the first possible moment after all objects that can pick up the parameter have been created. In our case, this means that we call the method in the constructor of the class KTsp after we have created an instance of TspGda.

[3] *If you always get the default value, although the configuration file has been saved correctly, you have most likely misspelled the group or the parameter name.*

6

KTsp Matures

It's time to give KTsp more functionality. In this chapter, we add the standard functions of a KDE program to KTsp.

6.1 Progress Indicators for "Long" Actions

If the computer needs more than a few seconds to do something, the user should be informed about the current progress. It's extraordinarily frustrating for users to sit in front of a "silent" computer without knowing whether the program has crashed or why it isn't doing anything (or at least "seems" to be doing nothing). For actions that take some time, you can set up a dialog box to give progress feedback by using QProgressDialog.

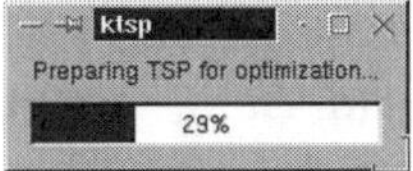

Figure 6.1 *A QProgressDialog.*

To get an idea about how this all works, set a large number of points in Preferences, TSP Preferences. When you start the program, quite a long time will pass before the actual optimization begins. As currently set, we do inform the user about the point from which we are currently calculating the neighbor, but that's not enough. We want to make the whole thing more user friendly, and we can do so by using QProgressDialog.

Install ktsp-0.0.7.tgz from the New Riders website. Configure KTsp for 1,000 points and start the optimization of a TSP. While the neighbors are calculated, a small dialog box appears, just like the box shown in Figure 6.1. As long as the cursor is over KTsp (but not over the progress dialog), it will transform itself into a watch to show that KTsp is currently doing something time intensive. However, the program stays responsive.

We lazy programmers can be quite glad that we get this handy feature with only a few lines of code in `KTsp::slotStart()`:

```
void KTsp::slotStart()
  {
  QProgressDialog dlg( i18n( "Preparing TSP for"
                             "optimization..." ),
                       0,
                       tsp->numberOfPoints(),
                       this,
                       "Progress Dialog" );
connect( tsp, SIGNAL( progressNeighbours( int ) ),
         &dlg, SLOT( setProgress( int ) ) );
tsp->startTsp( _runs );
}
```

Because the progress bar is needed only as long as the program execution is in `slotStart()`, we can create it on the stack. The passed parameters mean the following, one after another: The first parameter is a string that is shown in the dialog box. The second parameter is a string serving as the text on the Cancel button in the dialog. We don't want such a button, so we just pass a null pointer. The third parameter is the maximal value for the progress, which is 100%. In our case, it is the number of points. The fourth parameter specifies the parent, and the fifth the Qt internal name of the instance of this dialog box. The next line connects the signal `progressNeighbours()`, which is sent by TspGda with the slot `setProgress()` of QProgressDialog.

Because the signal `progressNeighbours()` has already been sent by TspGda so that the status bar can be adjusted, these two lines are sufficient for us to create a progress dialog.

A difficult task with progress indicators is to know how long something will really take. As mentioned earlier, users will be annoyed when sitting in front of computers without any clue whether a program is doing anything. Likewise, users will be annoyed by a progress dialog that blinks for a quarter of a second only and then disappears, before the user can actually read any of the information. Try it with KTsp. Set a small number of points. A "small" number depends on the speed of your computer. Start with 50. No progress dialog will pop up upon start of an optimization.

QProgressDialog uses the first few calls of `setProgress()` to guess how long the whole action will take. If the result is less than the minimal time, the dialog box won't display. Four seconds are preset as the minimal time; by calling `setMinimumDuration()`, you can adjust the value to your needs. To prevent misunderstandings, the QProgressDialog doesn't wait the four seconds until it appears, but it calculates the presumed total time. If it's more than four seconds, it will be displayed onscreen; if it's less, it won't be displayed. That's a very nice property.

If a "long action" is keeping Qt from processing events, the progress bar won't be updated either. Luckily, KTsp version 0.0.2 has taken care of that already: We just call `kapp->processEvents()` from time to time. Otherwise it wouldn't have been possible to pass information about the status of the program along to the main window. Basically, there's a rule for every KDE program: If something might be time intensive, `kapp->procesEvents()` has to be called in between; otherwise, the GUI will "hang." The word *might* is important. Most things are taken care of quickly, but sometimes they can last longer. A short file, for example, can be loaded very quickly, but the programmer can't know whether the file is on the local hard drive. Perhaps it's on a disk that has been included in the local file system with NFS. Because traffic in the network could be high, the small file might take quite some time.

6.2 Loading of TSPs

So far, we've only worked with TSPs that have been generated with random numbers. That's not enough for the workshop manager who wants an optimization for the treatment of his work pieces. He wants to load real-world tasks in the program and achieve results that are hopefully better than the current ones. Therefore, we need to enable KTsp to load and save TSPs.

What is the TSP file format supposed to look like? We could just write all coordinates of the points one after the other in a binary file. We need to keep in mind, however, that the binary representation of numbers is not the same on every computer system. Because the user should be able to exchange TSPs between the computer on which KTsp runs and the machine that treats the work pieces, we need a format that every computer can read.

ASCII is the only thing left. Now the decision isn't hard anymore. Every point is specified through exactly two numbers (the coordinates). We write those numbers as a string one after the other, one per line, beginning with the X value. An odd number of values shows that the file is corrupted. Empty lines are ignored. Everything behind a pound sign (#) is a comment. We add a header so that the file can be identified as a TSP; the header also contains the version number of the file format. Later format versions can be designed so that they can be directly inserted as programs to the machines. As the file extension, we use .tsp.

With this, the file format is finished:

```
# TSP file
# Version 1.0
```

```
10.48375466584
0.00948473248
7.30950243054888
1127.394732645859587
```

More points would exist in a real TSP file. The file could look like this, and would still be valid:

```
# TSP file
# Version 1.0

# Point 1
9.23493759845845         # X
1.3647374764754   # y

# Point 2
20.60234755425#X
87.4987435945     # Y   maybe wrong

# This file is too short
```

The file looks pretty unorganized, and it is actually. However, it represents a correct TSP file according to the preceding specifications. We just have to filter out all the uninteresting stuff while loading. Before you start with the actual loading process, you should install ktsp-0.0.7.tgz (from the New Riders website).

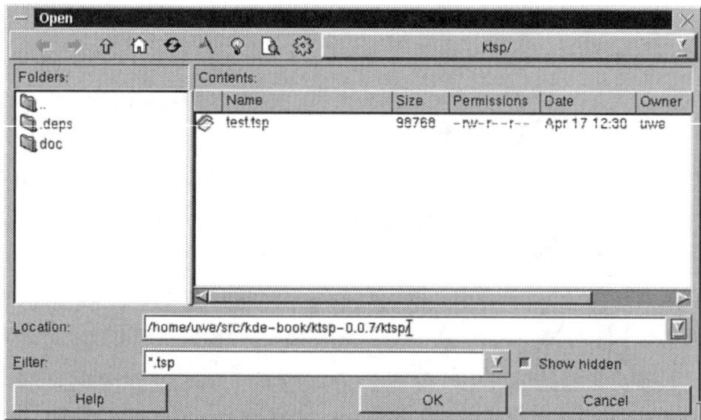

Figure 6.2 *A File dialog box (another gift for the lazy programmer).*

Now click on File, Open or on the corresponding icon on the toolbar. You should see the file dialog box KFileDialog, like the one shown in Figure 6.2.[1] This extraordinary flexible dialog box is another present from

[1] *The display could be different on your computer because the KDE File dialog box can be configured to a very high extent by using the wheel on the toolbar. I prefer to look at directories and files separate from each other.*

KDE; the lazy programmer doesn't have to worry about how such a dialog box is created. Users can customize it just as they want to.

A TSP test file test.tsp in the directory ktsp-0.0.7/ktsp serves as an example. Navigate the File dialog box to the correct directory and load test.tsp. The TSP will be loaded. If you don't have an extremely fast computer, you'll see the progress dialog while the TSP is prepared for the optimization. Play around a little bit with the loading function. Enter a nonexistent file or change the access rights of test.tsp so that it can't be read anymore. KTsp will in any case show an understandable message.

Now to the source. The changes in the class declaration of KTsp aren't really anything new. Let's immediately review the implementation:

```
void KTsp::slotOpen()
  {
  while ( dirty ) queryUnsaved();
  QString name = KFileDialog::getOpenFileName( 0, "*.tsp",
                                               this,
                                              "Open Dialog" );
  if ( name.isEmpty() ) return;
  QFile file( name );
  if ( !file.exists() )
    {
    showFileError( i18n( "The requested file "
                         "does not exist!" ) );
    return;
    }
  tsp->startTsp( name, _runs );
  }
```

In the *while* loop, we ask the users whether they want to save an optimized (but so far unsaved) TSP until they actually save it or answer "No." In the latter case, the data would be lost.

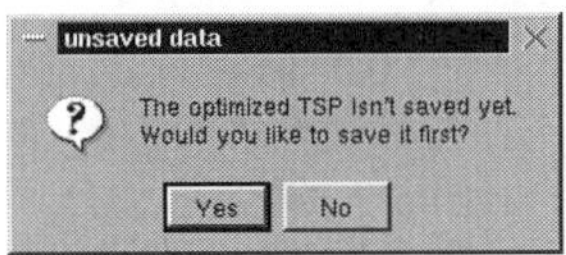

Figure 6.3 *A protection against losing data.*

The corresponding dialog box looks like that shown in Figure 6.3. The dialog box asks whether the TSP should be saved. The Yes button is the default button. If the user just presses the Return key, the program will save the TSP. That's something we have to get used to: The default button is always the one that can do the least damage. The member function `queryUnsaved()` just opens KMsgBox and returns, corresponding to which button has been clicked by the user, true or false. Because we need functionality at other places as well (for example, `slotQuit()`), it is packed in a method that can be called. The implementation is fairly simple:

```
void KTsp::queryUnsaved()
  {
  int rc = KMsgBox::yesNo( this, i18n( "unsaved data" ),
              i18n( "The optimized TSP isn't"
                 "saved yet.\n"
                 "Would you like"
                 "to save it first?" ),
              KMsgBox::QUESTION | KMsgBox::DB_FIRST );
  if ( rc == 2 )
    {
    dirty = false;
    return;
    }
  slotSaveAs();
  }
```

`KMsgBox::yesNo()` is a KMsgBox static member function that can be directly called and instantly creates an instance of the class. Its return value is the number of the clicked button. The first parameter specifies KTsp as the parent of the dialog box. The second one is the text, which will display in the title bar or the dialog box. The third one sets the text that displays in the dialog box. With the fourth, we see that the dialog box displays a question mark and that the first button (Yes) is the default one. If the user clicks on the second button (No), the flag `dirty` will be set to false, meaning that there's no unsaved data left. Otherwise, we call `slotSaveAs()`. The method saves either the TSP and then sets dirty to false, or fails and dirty will remain true.

Back to `slotOpen()`. After we've either saved or skipped the old optimized TSP, we open a KFileDialog with the static member function `KFileDialog:getOpenFileName()`. The return value is a QString containing the whole filename, including the path. `QString::isEmpty()` returns true in two cases: If the string is empty, it'll happen if the user deletes the whole line `"Location"`. Second, if the string is NULL, this happens if the user clicks on the Cancel button. In both cases, nothing is left for `slotOpen()` to do, so we just leave the method.

During the next step, we create an instance of QFile with the filename as the parameter for the constructor. QFile is an object that will save us a lot of work while dealing with files.[2] In this case, we'll use only QFile to check whether the file actually exists. If it does not, we'll just display the message

[2] *I want to urge the lazy programmer to take a look at QFile and the similar objects such as QTextStream and QFileInfo in the Qt online documentation. It can save a lot of code.*

box informing the user about it and leave `slotOpen()`. If the file exists, we'll pass its name to `TspGda::startTsp()`.

The file has neither been read nor opened so far. TspGda passes only the name through to TspIO, which knows how to generate a TSP from a file that can then be processed by TspGda. `TspIO::loadTsp()` is a slightly longer method, which we need to take a closer look at:

```
Point *TspIO::loadTsp( QString name, int neighbours )
  {
  Point *p = 0;
  Point *tmp = 0;
  QFile file( name );
  QFileInfo info( file );
  if ( info.isDir() ) return p;
  if ( file.open( IO_ReadOnly ) )
    {
    QTextStream stream( &file );
    QString line;
    bool ok;
    int numLines = 0;
    int numPoints = 0;
    while ( !stream.eof() )
      {
      line = stream.readLine();
      numLines++;
      }
    // there can't be more points in that TSP than

    // half the number of lines
    tmp = new Point[numLines / 2];
    CHECK_PTR( tmp );
    numLines = 0;
    file.at( 0 );
```

It returns a pointer to a TSP and gets the filename and the wanted number of neighbors as parameters. If the returned pointer is a null pointer, the file hasn't been read successfully.

`LoadTsp()` creates an instance of QFile, too, with the filename as the parameter of the constructor and an instance of `QFileInfo` with the QFile as parameter. `QFileInfo` can give us plenty of information about the file. In this case, we'll be interested in whether it's a directory or not. If so, we'll leave `loadTsp()` and return a null pointer because a directory surely isn't a TSP. The next step will be to open the file, to read it, and to create a `QTextStream` if the opening is successful.

We've chosen an array as the internal data structure for a TSP because this structure provides advantages for the assignment of neighbors and points. We face a dilemma, however, when we load the data from a file. We have to create the array, although we don't know how big it has to be before we load the points. Luckily, the file format that we have chosen provides a hint. Every point requires two lines in a file. In addition there's the header and the comments or empty lines. With this information, we can guess the upper bound for the number of the points. The largest number possible is half of all lines in the files. Correspondingly, we count all lines, without actually analyzing the data, and create an array that can take half as many points. You can be pretty sure that this structure is too big, but it can never be too small. Setting the reading pointer back to the beginning of the file by calling `file.at( 0 )` is our next step:

```
// Check the two lines in the header
if ( stream.eof() )
  {
  delete [] tmp;
  file.close();
  return p;
  }
line = stream.readLine();
if ( !isTsp( line ) )
  {
  delete [] tmp;
  file.close();
  return p;
  }

if ( stream.eof() )
  {
  delete [] tmp;
  file.close();
  return p;
  }
line = stream.readLine();
if ( !isCorrectVersion( line ) )
  {
  delete [] tmp;
  file.close();
  return p;
  }
```

Before the actual reading of the data begins, we'll check the header to determine whether the file is a TSP and whether the version of the file format is known by this KTsp version. If either test fails, we'll delete the array and leave `loadTsp()` by returning a null pointer to show that the file hasn't been read successfully.

```
// now read the data
    while ( !stream.eof() )
      {
      line = stream.readLine();
      if ( !ignore( line ) )
        {
        if ( ( numLines % 2 ) == 0 )
```

```
            {
            // even line number = x value
            tmp[numPoints].setX( line.toDouble( &ok ) );
            }
          else
            {
            // odd line number = y value
            tmp[numPoints].setY( line.toDouble( &ok ) );
            numPoints++;
            }
          numLines++;
          }
      }
```

In this part, `loadTsp()` actually reads the data. Soon, we'll have to take a close look at the member function `ignore()`. It removes all unnecessary whitespaces and comments from the line, and returns false if data is left or true if it's an empty line that `loadTsp()` should ignore.

We convert the content of the line into a number by calling `QString::toDouble()` and assigning it as the *X* value of the current point if it's an even number or as the *Y* value if it's an odd number. `QString::toDouble()` tells us whether any problems with conversion have occurred by the passed bool variable. With further analysis of this bool, we would gain further information about whether the file is corrupted. I've left that step out, however, so as not to blow up `loadTsp()` even more. (Implementing this on your own might be a good exercise in learning more about the Qt classes we are using here.) All data has now been read:

```
  // all points read
      if ( ( numLines % 2 ) == 1 )
        {
        // Oops! File was corrupt
        // p is still a null pointer, we just have to
        // delete tmp
        delete [] tmp;
        }
      else
        {
        // let's cut the data structure down to its real
        // size and prepare everything for returning the TSP
        p = new Point[numPoints];
        CHECK_PTR( p );
        _numberOfNeighbours = neighbours;
        if ( _numberOfNeighbours >= numPoints )
                      _numberOfNeighbours = numPoints - 1;
```

If the number of read lines (without the ignored ones) is odd, the file must have been corrupted. In this case, we'll free the memory that our array is using. At the end of the method, we'll return a null pointer.

In the case of an even number of lines , we'll assume that we have a valid TSP. Now that we finally know the number of points, we can reduce the size of our data structure to the correct size. However, new and `realloc()` don't get along with each other very well. To save memory in the long run, we unfortunately have to allocate more memory for a short period of time. We can create a new array of the correct size, copy the points into it, and delete the old one. The number of the neighbors could also be too large. The number of neighbors always has to be less than the number of points. We could have a small TSP with 12 points, but 18 neighbors. If that's the case, we must adjust the number of neighbors:

```
        for ( int i = 0; i < numPoints; i++ )
          {
          p[i].setX( tmp[i].x() );
          p[i].setY( tmp[i].y() );
          p[i].setForwardI( i + 1 );
          p[i].setForwardP( &(p[i+1]) );
          p[i].setBackwardI( i - 1 );
          p[i].setBackwardP( &(p[i-1]) );
          p[i].setDirectionForward( true );
          p[i].setNumberOfNeighbours( _numberOfNeighbours );
          }
        // correct the first and last one
        p[0].setBackwardI( numPoints - 1 );
        p[0].setBackwardP( &(p[numPoints-1]) );
        p[numPoints-1].setForwardI( 0 );
        p[numPoints-1].setForwardP( &(p[0]) );
        delete[] tmp;
        _numberOfPoints = numPoints;
        _numberOfNeighbours = neighbours;
        }
      file.close();
      }
    else
      {
      // could not open file
      // p is still a null pointer => nothing to do
      }
    return p;
    }
```

In the last part of `loadTsp()`, we copy all the points from the old array into the new one and initiate them. The old array won't be needed anymore and will be deleted with Delete. Finally, we'll return a pointer to the data structure or a null pointer in case we couldn't read the file correctly into a TSP. We still have to take a look at the member function `ignore()`:

```
bool TspIO::ignore( QString s )
  {
  int i = s.find( '#' );
  if ( i >= 0 ) s.truncate( i );
```

```
QString tmp = s.simplifyWhiteSpace();
// We removed a possible comment and removed all white spaces
// at the begin and end of the string. All white spaces inside
// the string have been converted to single spaces.
// Numbers can't contain spaces so the remaining string is
// either empty or a number.
s = tmp;
return s.isEmpty();
}
```

If there's a comment in the line, we cut it with `QString::truncate()` where it begins. `QString::simplifyWhiteSpace()` removes all whitespaces at the beginning and at the end of the string. Every series of whitespaces within the string is converted into one white space. After we've taken care of whitespaces in the line, it should contain exactly one number or an empty line. Correspondingly, the return value of `QString::isEmpty()` is exactly the value needed by `ignore()`: True if the line is supposed to be ignored; false if it contains the coordinate of a point.

The corresponding part of `TspGda::startTsp()` looks pretty simple:

```
emit statusChanged( KTsp::STATUSBAR_LOADING );
kapp->processEvents();
Point *pTemp = io->loadTsp( name, _confNumberOfNeighbours );
if ( pTemp == 0 )
  {
  emit statusChanged( KTsp::STATUSBAR_LOAD_ERROR );
  return;
  }
checkOldTsp();
points = pTemp;
```

First, `startTsp()` sends the signal `statusChanged()` to inform the GUI part about the loading of the file. We have to allow Qt to take care of the message queue before we start loading the file so that the `paint event` gets to the status bar.[3] In the next line, TspIO loads the file. If `startTsp()` gets a null pointer back, it will send the signal `statusChanged()` to inform the GUI about the failure and return. After successfully loading the file, `checkOldTsp()` deletes all the currently existing data structures and replaces the structure with the new TSP. The next steps are just like we're used to after generating the TSP.

There's one thing left to talk about: how the GUI part reacts to the Signals. The corresponding part of `KTsp::slotStatusChanged()` shows it:

3 *An annotation to clear up some misunderstandings: The sending and receiving of Qt signals doesn't have anything to do with the event queue. Slots connected to signals will work just fine even if* `kapp->processEvents()` *is blocked. However, we want the GUI to react to our signal and change the display in the status bar. The status bar will have to be redrawn. That's why it's necessary to call* `kapp->processEvents()`.

```
case STATUSBAR_LOADING:
      statusBar()->changeItem( i18n( "Loading..." ), 0 );
      break;

case STATUSBAR_SAVING:
      statusBar()->changeItem( i18n( "Saving..." ), 0 );
      break;

case STATUSBAR_LOAD_ERROR:
      statusBar()->changeItem( i18n( "Loading error" ), 0 );
      showFileError( i18n( "Unable to read the requested file.\n" ) );

      statusBar()->changeItem( i18n( "Ready" ), 0 );
      break;
```

There is only one case that deals with errors that isn't totally trivial. The display in the status bar is set to `"Loading error"` first, and then `showFileError()` displays a KMsgBox that informs the user about the problem as well. When the user closes the box, the text in the status bar will be changed to `"Ready"` and the program is ready for new tasks.

6.3 Saving of Solutions

It's always easier to write on a hard disk than to read from it. The writing operations themselves aren't easier at all, but we can rightfully make a couple more assumptions while writing than we can while reading. If a program is written somewhat cleanly, the data will be what it's supposed to be. A TSP within the program is really a TSP; nobody could have renamed a KOffice document to the name of a TSP. It's different while reading. The coordinates of a point within the program are real numbers that represent the coordinates of a point. When reading, we have to take into account that somebody might have modified the file and corrupted it. That's not possible while writing.

Correspondingly, the code is a lot shorter. Before we take a look at it, let's answer the question why KTsp only knows a Save As function and not a Save function. In a text editor, users sometimes write something that grows with time. Sometimes they even write on it for several days. It would make sense that Save overwrites the old version with the new one without a query (and perhaps creates a backup of the old one). It's not what we want in KTsp. We don't want to overwrite the original version with the optimized one. Maybe we'll need the original again. That's why Save doesn't make any sense in this program. We would have to include a query whether the user really wants to overwrite the existing file anyway—and that's not what the users expect from Save.

Let's deal with `slotSaveAs()` first:

```
void KTsp::slotSaveAs()
  {
  QString name = KFileDialog::getSaveFileName( 0, "*.tsp",
                                               this,
                                               "Save Dialog" );
  if ( name.isEmpty() ) return;
  QFile file( name );
  if ( file.exists() )
    {
    int rc = KMsgBox::yesNo( this, i18n( "File exists" ),
                             i18n( "The file already
                                   "exists.\n"
                                   "Overwrite it?" ),
                           KMsgBox::QUESTION | KMsgBox::DB_SECOND );
    if ( rc == 2 ) return;
    }
  if ( tsp->saveTsp( name ) ) dirty = false;
  }
```

At the beginning, we get a name for the file from `KFileDialog`. Next, we check whether it's an empty name and leave the method in this case. If the file already exists, we'll ask the user with KMsgBox whether the file should be overwritten. If the user is against it, we'll leave the method. If the user is for it, we'll pass the name to `TspGda::saveTsp()`, which passes the request through to `TspIO`. `TspGda::saveTsp()`'s return value will tell us whether the action has been successful so that we can immediately set dirty to false. This part equals `slotOpen()` except that it doesn't take care of the unsaved data. The actual saving routine `TspIO::saveTsp()` is a lot easier than the reading routine:

```
bool TspIO::saveTsp( QString name, Point *tsp, int points )
  {
  QFile file( name );
  if ( !file.open( IO_WriteOnly ) ) return false;
  QTextStream stream( &file );
  stream.precision( 60 );
  stream << "# TSP file\n";
  if ( file.status() != IO_Ok )
    {
    file.close();
    return false;
    }
  stream << "# Version 1.0\n";
  if ( file.status() != IO_Ok )
    {
    file.close();
    return false;
    }
  Point *p = tsp;
  do
    {
    stream << p->x() << "\n";
```

```
    stream << p->y() << "\n\n";
    if ( file.status() != IO_Ok )
      {
      file.close();
      return false;
      }
    p = p->nextPointer();
    } while ( p != tsp );
  file.close();
  return true;
  }
```

Just as with the reading, we create a QFile with the filename as the parameter for the constructor and open a file for writing with `QFile::open()`. If the opening fails, `saveTsp()` will be left with the return value false. If it has been successful, we'll create a `QTextStream` for the file and set its precision to 60 digits so that `QTextStream` converts numbers into strings as accurately as possible. Now that we have opened the file, both the header lines are written into it. If an error occurs, we'll leave `saveTsp()` with false. The loop writes first the *X* and the *Y* coordinate for every point in the TSP. After the *Y* value, we insert an empty line to give the file a more structured look. At the end, we close the file and return true. `TspGda::saveTsp()` is even easier:

```
bool TspGda::saveTsp( QString name )
  {
  emit statusChanged( KTsp::STATUSBAR_SAVING );
  if ( !io->saveTsp( name, bestPoints, _numberOfPoints ) )
    {
    emit statusChanged( KTsp::STATUSBAR_SAVE_ERROR );
    return false;
    }
  else
    {
    emit statusChanged( KTsp::STATUSBAR_READY );
    return true;
    }
  }
```

The member function sends the signal to indicate that the writing process has started; passes the task through to `TspIO::saveTsp()`; and informs the GUI part corresponding to the returned value about the success or failure by sending the signal `statusChanged()` and returning true or false.

6.4 We Can Do This Over FTP On the Internet, Too

Now that KTsp can read and write TSPs, we remember that KDE promises network transparency. Knowing this possibility, it's fair to assume that KTsp could operate over the Internet via FTP. The program has to learn to deal with URLs. It doesn't have to understand anything about the FTP protocol, however, because kfm (KDE's File Manager) provides this service to all KDE applications.

Install ktsp-0.0.8.tgz. File, Open presents the File dialog box in the normal manner. This time, the user can insert URLs such as `ftp://ftp.sysex.com.` na/pub/ktsp/test.tsp[4] in the input line "Location" and get the TSP that I've uploaded for testing purposes to the public FTP server. If you own a LAN, you can test this function in it, too. For a fuller understanding, we need to take a look at `slotOpen()` again:

```
void KTsp::slotOpen()
  {
  while ( dirty ) queryUnsaved();
  QString url = KFileDialog::getOpenFileURL( 0, "*.tsp",
                                             this,
                                             "Open Dialog" );
  loadFile( url );
  }
```

First, the method has become a lot smaller. That's because I have given most of the functionality to the method `KTsp::loadFile()`, because we'll need it at another time, too. The only real change is the usage of `KFileDialog::getOpenFileURL()` rather than `KFileDialog::getOpenFileName()`. Both dialog boxes look the same for the user. The only difference is that URLs can be used now. We pass the URL, which we get from `KFileDialog`, to the member function `loadFile()`, which takes care of the actual work:

```
void KTsp::loadFile( QString url )
  {
  QString name = "";
  if ( url.isEmpty() ) return;
  if ( !KFM::download( url, name ) )
    {
    return;
    }
  QFile file( name );
  if ( !file.exists() )
    {
    showFileError( i18n( "The requested file does not exist!" ) );
    return;
    }
  disableOpenNew();
  tsp->startTsp( name, _runs );
  KFM::removeTempFile( name );
  enableOpenNew();
  }
```

The more interesting method is `KFM::download()` to which the two QStrings are passed as parameters. The first one contains the URL, which

---

4 *No, it is not sy-sex; it's sys-ex!*

`KFileDialog` provided, the second one is empty. Notice that we don't differ between a local and non-local file. In the case of a local file, kfm converts the URL in the first QString into a filename and returns it in the second QString. If we're dealing with a non-local file, kfm will download it via FTP and save it locally as a temporary file, which will be returned in the second QString. The downloading process is totally transparent for our program. In every case, it can deal with a file that can be loaded just like any other one. `KFM::download()` will return true if successful or false if not.

Finally, we need to clean up a bit and delete the temporary file by calling `KFM::removeTempFile()`. "Stop, stop! The file with the name 'name' will be deleted unconditionally. It could be a local file and not a temporary file." No worries! `KFM::removeTempFile()` deletes only temporary files created by `KFM::download()`. The user doesn't have to take care of it.

With a few lines and the help of kfm, we added local hard-disk and network support (even for the "net of the nets"). There's only one little feature missing for loading the TSPs.

6.5 Drag and Drop, Too

No modern desktop can get along without drag and drop (DnD). KDE knows DnD, so why doesn't KTsp? Drag a file out of kfm or directly from the desktop and drop it on KTsp. It won't matter whether it's a local or non-local file. As long as kfm supports the corresponding protocol, KTsp will "inherit" it.

Once again, a few lines of code are enough. First we consider the constructor of KTsp:

```
void KTsp::setupDND()
  {
  // create a drop zone over the whole main window and connect
  // it to slotDrop()
  KDNDDropZone *zone = new KDNDDropZone( this, DndURL );
  CHECK_PTR( zone );
  connect( zone, SIGNAL( dropAction( KDNDDropZone *) ),
           this, SLOT( slotDrop( KDNDDropZone * ) ) );
  }
```

The constructor calls `KTsp::setupDND()`. We create an area that accepts "drops" over the whole main window. The first parameter of `KDNDDropZone()` specifies our KTMW as the parent of the area. The second one tells it to accept URLs. The signal saying that something has been dropped on our area gets connected to the slot `slotDrop()` of KTsp. The information is put to use in the following way:

```
void KTsp::slotDrop( KDNDDropZone *drop )
  {
  if ( cannotOpen )
    {
```

```
    // we don't accept another TSP while an optimization
    // is running
    KMsgBox box( this,
                 i18n( "Drop error" ),
                 i18n( "Busy optimizing.\n"
                       "Cannot accept another TSP" ),
                 KMsgBox::EXCLAMATION,
                 i18n( "Dismiss" ) );
    box.exec();
    return;
    }
  while( dirty ) queryUnsaved();
  // we can't handle more than one TSP at a time
  // therefor we just take the first one
  QString url = drop->getURLList().first();
  loadFile( url );
  }
```

If KTsp is currently busy optimizing a TSP, it will reject the URL and inform the user with a KMsgBox. KTsp can take care of only one TSP, so we pass only the first URL in the list to `loadFile()` where it will be treated just like a URL from `KFileDialog`. If your program works with multiple URLs, you can use the whole list.

KDE gives us the FTP protocol as a present, like it gives us DnD. KDE hides all these small details for the lazy application programmer. So ends this discussion about all the loading and saving procedures. It's time to learn some new things.

6.6 Facelifting

Some basic remarks: KTsp contains all the functionality needed for the first release, but the main window doesn't really look like a classic example for a GUI program. It presents only the text and appears rather boring. The data in the main window must be presented graphically.

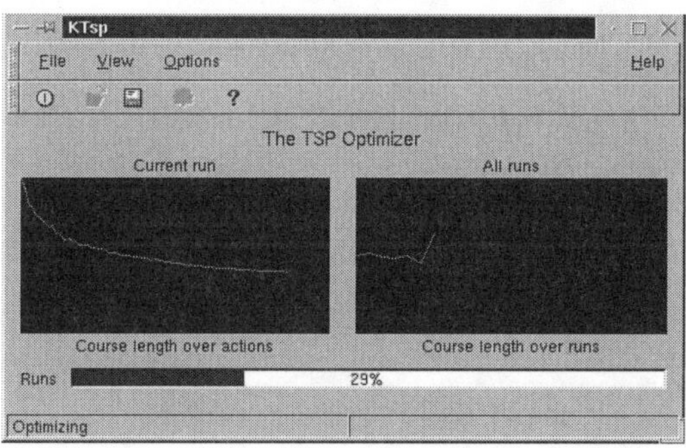

Figure 6.4 *The new face of KTsp.*

Install ktsp-0.0.9.tgz. If you start the program and start the optimization of a TSP, a window like that shown in Figure 6.4 will appear. The TSP menu is gone because it was unnecessary. It had only one item, the creation of a random TSP. This item belongs to the File menu. Beside the standard elements such as menubar, toolbar, and statusbar, the main window contains three new elements:

- A widget displaying the length of the circuit during an optimization run. It is updated frequently.
- A widget displaying the length of the circuit after every run. It is updated after every run.
- A progress bar displaying how many runs have been finished.

Although the new KTsp actually provides less information about the progress of the optimization for the users, the visualization is "more exciting." The size of the main window can be customized; the widgets adjust themselves to the new size. However, it can't fall short of its minimum size. Besides that, however, the main window can be resized. As you might have guessed, Qt layout managers in the background provide this flexibility. Let's take a look at how it has been realized:

```
void KTsp::setupView()
  {
  // The toplevel vertical layout
  QVBoxLayout *layout = new QVBoxLayout( w );
  CHECK_PTR( layout );

  // a horizontal layout for both displays
  QHBoxLayout *hlayout = new QHBoxLayout();
  CHECK_PTR( hlayout );

  // a QLabel for the headline
  QLabel *label = new QLabel( i18n( "The TSP Optimizer" ),
                              w, "Headline" );
  QFont f = label->font();
  f.setPointSize( f.pointSize() + 2 );
  label->setFont( f );
  label->setMinimumSize( label->sizeHint() );
  label->setAlignment( AlignCenter );

  // into the toplevel layout with them
  layout->addSpacing( 10 );
  layout->addWidget( label, 0 );
  layout->addSpacing( 5 );
  layout->addLayout( hlayout, 30 );
  layout->addSpacing( 10 );

  // construct the display for course length over actions
  aDisplay = new ActionsDisplay( w, "Actions Graph" );
```

```
CHECK_PTR( aDisplay );
connect( tsp, SIGNAL( quality( double ) ),
         aDisplay, SLOT( slotNextValue( double ) ) );
connect( tsp, SIGNAL( newRun() ),
         aDisplay, SLOT( slotClearDisplay() ) );

// construct the display for course length over runs
rDisplay = new RunsDisplay( w, "Runs Graph" );
CHECK_PTR( rDisplay );
connect( tsp, SIGNAL( currentQuality( double ) ),
         rDisplay, SLOT( slotNextValue( double ) ) );

// into the horizontal layout with them
hlayout->addSpacing( 10 );
hlayout->addWidget( aDisplay );
hlayout->addSpacing( 20 );
hlayout->addWidget( rDisplay );
hlayout->addSpacing( 10 );

// a new horizontal layout for the progress bar
// that goes into the toplevel layout
hlayout = new QHBoxLayout();
CHECK_PTR( hlayout );
layout->addLayout( hlayout, 1 );
layout->addSpacing( 20 );

// a QLabel informing what the progress bar is for
label = new QLabel( i18n( "Runs" ), w, "Runs Progress" );
CHECK_PTR( label );
label->setMinimumSize( label->sizeHint() );

// the progress bar itself
progressBar = new QProgressBar( w, "Runs Progress Bar" );
CHECK_PTR( progressBar );
connect( tsp, SIGNAL( currentRun( int ) ),
         progressBar, SLOT( setProgress( int ) ) );

// into the horizontal layout with them
hlayout->addSpacing( 10 );
hlayout->addWidget( label, 0 );
hlayout->addSpacing( 10 );
hlayout->addWidget( progressBar, 1 );
hlayout->addSpacing( 10 );

// finally, we activate layout management
layout->activate();
}
```

The KTsp constructor calls `KTsp::setupView()`. First, we create a `QVBoxLayout` as the main layout with the main widget ("main view") of KTMW as the parent. We insert the other widgets and subordinated layouts in it. We already know about `QLayout`, so I don't need to explain the code in depth.

It's worth mentioning that the first `QHBoxLayout`, containing both of the graphics displays, gets a stretch factor of 30; the second one, containing the `QLabel` and the `QProgressBar`, gets a stretch factor of 1. This ensures that the progress bar changes its size only very little, while the graphical displays get most of the size changes.

The graphics displays, just as the progress bar, get connected to the corresponding signals of TspGda so that the display will be updated if needed.

We need to talk about a limitation of KTMW. In our case, the main view of KTMW is a QWidget containing the other widgets. A QWidget itself doesn't provide a reasonable minimal size by itself. It shouldn't be a problem for us because the main layout takes care of it. The problem is KTMW not caring about this minimal size.[5] We have to find another solution. We can set the minimal size with `setMinimumSize()` right after the creation of the main view at the beginning of the constructor. Although this works pretty well for KTsp, it is still nothing more than a hack that won't take care of different font types and sizes. We will have to live with it until KDE 2.0 is released.

The graphics displays in the main window have the types `ActionsDisplay` and `RunsDisplay`. They're derived from the base type `GraphDisplay`. Before we deal with `GraphDisplay`, we want to take a look at the widget Graph, which is the main component of GraphDisplay. The declaration of Graph is as follows:

```
class Graph : public QWidget
  {
  Q_OBJECT

  public:
    Graph( QWidget *parent = 0, const char *name = 0 );
    virtual ~Graph();
    virtual QSize sizeHint() const;
    // clears the display and resets all data
    void clear();
    // sets the vertical scale of the display
    void setVScale( double v );
    // sets the horizontal scale of the display
    void setHScale( int h );

  public slots:
    // the next value to be displayed
    void slotNextValue( double value );

  protected:
    // repaints the whole display
```

5 *The author of KTMW has promised to solve this problem in KDE 2.0*

```
    virtual void paintEvent( QPaintEvent *e );

  private:
    // internal store of the scales
    int hScale;
    double vScale;
    // number of received values
    int receivedValues;
    // storage of all values received so far
    QList<double> values;
  };
```

Graph is derived from QWidget. The two methods `setVScale()` and `setHScale()` set the largest possible value that can be displayed and, respectively, the possible numbers of values.

`Graph::slotNextValue()` draws the next value in the graphic and saves the value for future redrawns. `Graph::clear()` deletes the graphic along with all the saved points. We've overwritten the virtual method `paintEvent()` so that we can redraw our graphics in case the main window (and this widget) gets resized. The QList is the only interesting aspect of private elements. It is a template class whose instance we're using to save all values as doubles.

```
Graph::Graph( QWidget *parent, const char *name )
         : QWidget( parent, name )
  {
  vScale = 0.0;
  hScale = 0;
  receivedValues = 0;
  values.setAutoDelete( true );
  setBackgroundColour( black );
  setMinimumSize( 200, 100 );
  }
```

The constructor initiates all internal data. Apart from that, only two lines are of interest to us. As I was saying, QList should save the received data. Actually, it saves pointers to the data. So, the question arises: What will happen with the data if the instance of QList gets deleted or if `QList::clear()` is called? It's preset that `clear()` deletes the internal list of pointers, but not the data itself. The QList acts as if it doesn't own the data. That's not exactly what we need, because no other class is responsible for the data. We change the behavior with `QList::setAutoDelete( true )` so that the data gets deleted if something is deleted from the list. Second we set the minimal size of our graphic display with `Graph:setMinimumSize()`. We've chosen the values for width and height more or less at random to make sure that Graph can display the data reasonably, even when at its minimal size.

```
Graph::~Graph()
  {
  values.clear();
  }
```

We delete all data being saved in the QList in the destructor.

```
QSize Graph::sizeHint() const
  {
  return minimumSize();
  }
```

We overwrite the virtual method `sizeHint()` so that it returns the minimal size:

```
void Graph::clear()
  {
  erase();
  values.clear();
  receivedValues = 0;
  }
```

`Graph::clear()` erases the display with the inherited function from QWidget, `erase()`, meaning all pixels get the background colour. Next, we delete all data in the QList with `values.clear()` and set the number of received data to 0. In other words, Graph is getting prepared for a new set of data.

```
void Graph::setVScale( double v )
  {
  vScale = v;
  }

void Graph::setHScale( int h )
  {
  hScale = h;
  }
```

The two methods `setVScale()` and `setHScale()` are trivial. They save the passed values in the corresponding member variables:

```
void Graph::slotNextValue( double value )
  {
  if ( receivedValues >= hScale )
    {
    setHScale( hScale * 2 );
    update();
    }
  QPainter *painter = new QPainter( this );
  CHECK_PTR( painter );
  painter->setWindow( 0, 0, hScale, vScale );
  painter->setPen( red );
  if ( receivedValues == 0 )
    {
    painter->drawPoint( 0, vScale - value );
```

```
      }
    else
      {
      painter->drawLine( receivedValues - 1, vScale - *values.getLast(),
                         receivedValues, vScale - value );
      }
    delete painter;
    double *tmp = new double;
    CHECK_PTR( tmp );
    *tmp = value;
    values.append( tmp );
    receivedValues++;
    }
```

`Graph::setNextValue()` is more interesting. In many cases, we'll already know in advance about how much data will have to be displayed. This is unproblematic. What if we don't know the exact number? In that case, we must start with a reasonable value for the horizontal scale and if the number is too small, we'll have to make a new scale. The first *if* statement handles this. If the Graph has to display more data than foreseen, we'll double the horizontal scale and call the inherited method `update()`, erasing the widget, creating a "paint event," and leading to the call of `Graph::paintEvent()`. We'll deal with `paintEvent()` in a minute; the method redraws the widget corresponding to the new scale.

After the *if* statement, the drawing of the received data begins. Just like we're already used to, we create an instance of QPainter. `QPainter::setWindow()` handles the exact mapping of the values to the current size of the widget Graph. We set the brush colour to red. Now, we need to differ between the first and all other points. In the first case, we really draw a point. In all other cases, we draw a line from the last point to the current one. By subtracting the *Y* value of the point from `vScale`, we determine that the edge of the widget really corresponds to the *Y* value 0, and the upper one to the maximal *Y* value. Otherwise the graph would be reverted vertically.

After deleting the instance of QPainter, the received values still have to be saved in the QList. QList saves pointers to the data. That's why we create data of the type double on the heap, assign the correct value to it, and insert it into the list by calling `QList::append()`. We don't have to handle the freeing of the memory because we told QList to take care of it by itself. Finally, `receivedValues` has to be incremented. The Graph won't know how much data has been received unless we increment it.

All widgets inherit the virtual method `paintEvent()` from QWidget, which does nothing in its original implementation. It has to be overwritten to do something useful. If the widget or parts of it have to be redrawn, the method is called. If your X server doesn't support "double buffering," it will be necessary to redraw the widget (in case it has been covered by another one). Even with "double buffering" enabled, it's still possible that the X server doesn't have enough RAM left. The widget will also have to be redrawn, if it gets resized. The programmer doesn't have to take care of calling `paintEvent()`, Qt does it for us. On the other hand, Qt can't know how to correctly redraw the widget. The programmer must ensure the correct implementation:

```
void Graph::paintEvent( QPaintEvent * )
  {
  if ( receivedValues != 0 )
    {
    QPainter *painter = new QPainter( this );
    CHECK_PTR( painter );
    painter->setWindow( 0, 0, hScale, vScale );
    painter->setPen( red );

    double *tmp;
    double last;
    tmp = values.first();
    if ( tmp != 0 )
      {
      painter->drawPoint( 0, vScale - *tmp );
      last = *tmp;
      }
    tmp = values.next();

    for ( int i = 1; tmp != 0; tmp = values.next(), i++ )
      {
      painter->drawLine( i - 1, vScale - last,
                         i, vScale - *tmp );
      last = *tmp;
      }
    delete painter;
    }
  }
```

`paintEvent()` won't have anything to do if Graph hasn't received any data, because the background already has the corresponding colour. If there's already existing data, we'll draw the Graph just as we're used to, only this time with the data from the list. The interesting thing is that we don't care about the current size of the window, although it could have been resized. `QPainter::setWindow()` ensures that the values are always being illustrated correctly on the current size of the widget without us having to worry about it.

That's all about the class Graph. Now we must talk about the class `GraphDisplay`, another widget derived from QWidget that contains Graph:

```
class GraphDisplay : public QWidget
  {
  Q_OBJECT

  public:
    GraphDisplay( QString text1, QString text2,
                  QWidget *parent = 0, const char *name = 0 );
    ~GraphDisplay();

  protected:
    Graph *graph;
  };
```

The constructor takes two QStrings in addition to the normal parameters:

```
GraphDisplay::GraphDisplay( QString text1, QString text2,
                            QWidget *parent, const char *name )
     : QWidget( parent, name )
  {
  QVBoxLayout *layout = new QVBoxLayout( this );
  CHECK_PTR( layout );

  QLabel *label1 = new QLabel( text1, this );
  CHECK_PTR( label1 );
  label1->setMinimumSize( label1->sizeHint() );
  label1->setAlignment( AlignCenter );

  QLabel *label2 = new QLabel( text2, this );
  CHECK_PTR( label2 );
  label2->setMinimumSize( label2->sizeHint() );
  label2->setAlignment( AlignCenter );

  graph = new Graph( this );
  CHECK_PTR( graph );
  graph->setMinimumSize( graph->sizeHint() );

  layout->addWidget( label1, 0 );
  layout->addSpacing( 2 );
  layout->addWidget( graph, 1 );
  layout->addSpacing( 2 );
  layout->addWidget( label2, 0 );
  layout->activate();
  }
```

A `QVBoxLayout` is being created with the `GraphDisplay` as the parent. We create two QLabels by passing two QStrings to them and an instance of Graph. The three widgets are inserted into the layout: The first one is placed over the Graph as the title, and the second one below as the description. Both QLabels get a stretch factor of 0, Graph a stretch factor of 1. All changes to the size of `GraphDisplay` will affect only the Graph, not the QLabels. Finally, we activate the layout management for the `GraphDisplay`.

Because we created all three widgets with GraphDisplay as their parent, we don't need to care about their deletion.

`RunsDisplay` and `ActionsDisplay`, which are actually used by KTsp, are derived from this widget. First, take a look at the class declaration of `RunsDisplay`:

```
class RunsDisplay : public GraphDisplay
  {
  Q_OBJECT

  public:
    RunsDisplay( QWidget *parent = 0, const char *name = 0 );
    ~RunsDisplay();

  public slots:
    // prepares the widget for displaying a new
    // set of data
    void slotClearDisplay();
    // sets the number of values to be displayed
    void slotNumberOfRuns( int value );
    // displays the next value
    void slotNextValue( double value );

  protected:
    int receivedValues;
    double sock;
  };
```

The constructor and destructor don't have any surprises. The declarations of three slots follow:

`RunsDisplay::slotClearDisplay()` prepares the whole widget for the displaying of the data, and showing the optimization of a new TSP. The next slot `slotNumberOfRuns()` sets the horizontal scale of the display, which won't be a problem in this case because the number of data is known. `SlotNextValue()` passes the received data to the actual display. Let's take a look at the implementation:

```
RunsDisplay::RunsDisplay( QWidget *parent, const char *name )
      : GraphDisplay( i18n( "All runs" ),
                      i18n( "Course length over runs" ),
                      parent, name )
  {
  receivedValues = 0;
  }
```

The constructor passes the parameters to `GraphDisplay`, as well as the two texts for the QLabels of GraphDisplay. The number of received data is set to 0.

```
void RunsDisplay::slotClearDisplay()
  {
  graph->clear();
  receivedValues = 0;
  }
```

`RunsDisplay::setClearDisplay()` leaves it to `Graph::clear()` to clean up and sets the number of received data back to 0.

```
void RunsDisplay::slotNumberOfRuns( int value )
  {
  graph->setHScale( value );
  }
```

The slot `slotNumberOfRuns()` just passes its parameter through to `Graph::setHScale()`:

```
void RunsDisplay::slotNextValue( double value )
  {
  if ( receivedValues == 0 )
    {
    sock = 0.95 * value;
    graph->setVScale( 0.1 * value );
    }
  graph->slotNextValue( value - sock );
  receivedValues++;
  }
```

The third slot, `slotNextValue()`, is a little bit more interesting. The values received by this slot are the results of a completed optimization run. We can assume that they're all approximately the same. The differences are so small that we would get a horizontal line. That's why we use 95% of the first result as the base value that we'll subtract from every result. Ten percent of the first result provides the vertical scale of the display. Now, we'll get a graph around the middle line of the display, significantly showing the differences of the results. Further on, all values minus the base value are passed to `Graph::slotNextValue()`.

The class `ActionsDisplay` looks similar, but is not the same:

```
class ActionsDisplay : public GraphDisplay
  {
  Q_OBJECT

  public:
    ActionsDisplay( QWidget *parent = 0, const char *name = 0 );
    ~ActionsDisplay();

  public slots:
    // prepares the display for the next set
    // of data
    void slotClearDisplay();
```

```
    // displays the next value
    void slotNextValue( double value );

  protected:
    int receivedValues;
  };
```

Because it's impossible for KTsp to know how many actions will be needed to finish one optimizing run, `ActionsDisplay` doesn't contain a slot receiving such a value. Apart from that, the declaration is similar to the one of `RunsDisplay`. The constructor looks a little bit different, too:

```
ActionsDisplay::ActionsDisplay( QWidget *parent,
                                const char *name )
     : GraphDisplay( i18n( "Current run" ),
                     i18n( "Course length over actions" ),
                     parent, name )
  {
  graph->setHScale( 120 );
  receivedValues = 0;
  }
```

It differs from the constructor of `RunsDisplay` in that it sets the horizontal scale to 120, which is enough for most of the TSPs. If you want to see how Graph rescales itself during an optimization run, you should set the value to 60 (or some other value). You'll also have to change it in the slot `slotClearDisplay()`:

```
void ActionsDisplay::slotClearDisplay()
  {
  graph->clear();
  graph->setHScale( 120 );
  receivedValues = 0;
  }
```

This slot differs from its counterpart in RunsDisplay only by setting the scale to 120. The differences show more obviously in the slot `slotNextValue()`:

```
void ActionsDisplay::slotNextValue( double value )
  {
  switch ( receivedValues )
    {
    case 0:
      break;
    case 1:
      graph->setVScale( value );
    default:
      graph->slotNextValue( value );
      break;
    }
  receivedValues++;
  }
```

The differences between the values received by `ActionsDisplay` are significantly larger than the ones of `RunsDisplay`. That's why we don't have to use the trick with the "base value." However, once again, we have another problem coming up. The first result is the length of the non-optimized TSP. As a rule, this value is so large that it can't be used for the vertical scale. If we used it anyway, the graph would practically be invisible. We just skip it and use the second one for the scale. The missing break in the *case* statement isn't really missing. The value is used not only for the scale, but also to be displayed.

Along with the facelifting, we've added another small feature. Programs such as KWrite can be called with a command-line parameter. The program interprets it as a filename or an URL and tries to open the corresponding file. If you have a *.kdelnk file for a program on your desktop (or panel), you start the program by clicking on the icon. It has worked with KTsp, too. You can drop a file on the icon and the program will start and open the file. It'll only work, however, if your program understands the command-line parameter.

We want to include this useful property in KTsp, too. We need to make only a few changes:

```
int main( int argc, char* argv[] )
  {
  KApplication app( argc, argv, "KTsp" );
  QString s;
  if ( argc > 1 )
    {
    KURL *url = new KURL( argv[1] );
    CHECK_PTR( url );
    if ( url->isMalformed() )
      {
      s = QDir::currentDirPath();
      s += "/";
      s += argv[1];
      delete url;
      url = new KURL( s );
      }
    delete url;
    }
  KTsp *ktsp = new KTsp( s );
  CHECK_PTR( ktsp );
  ktsp->show();
  return app.exec();
  }
```

If `argc` is larger than 1 (meaning that the program has been called with parameters),[6] we interpret the first parameter as the filename or URL. We create an instance of KURL with the parameter. If KURL thinks that the URL is incorrect, it's probably a filename from the local directory without a path.[7] In this case, we create a name with the absolute path. After the *if* statement, the QString will either be empty or it will contain a valid URL that we can pass to the constructor.

The declaration of the KTsp constructor has to be changed to accept an argument:

```
KTsp( const char *fileName = 0 );
```

Before we take a look at the constructor to see how the URL is being handled, let's have a quick think: The constructor could just pass the URL to the method `KTsp::loadFile()`. At first look, it would really work. (Try it!) Let's remember `main()`. Such a procedure would mean that a TSP would be loaded and optimized before the constructor of KTsp finishes. The line `app->exec()` wouldn't have been run during the whole optimization. That leads to strange phenomenons. If you've really made this (trivial) change in KTsp, try to cancel the optimization after you have started KTsp with a valid filename as the command-line parameter!

It won't work to declare the method `KTsp::loadFile()` as public and to call it after `app.exec()` because the `app.exec()` will return only when the program terminates. Let's analyze the constructor to see how we can do it:

```
if ( fileName )
    {
    loadFileName = fileName;
    timer = new QTimer( this, "File Timer" );
    CHECK_PTR( timer );
    connect( timer, SIGNAL( timeout() ),
             this, SLOT( slotForcedLoad() ) );
    timer->start( 500, true );
    }
```

These lines are at the end of the constructor. If an URL is passed by the command line, we'll save it in the member variable `loadFileName` of KTsp. Now, we create a QTimer and connect its signal `timeout()` with the new slot `KTsp::slotForcedLoad()`. Next, the timer will be started with a timeout of half a second. If this time is over, the QTimer will send the signal

6 *KApplication or QApplication filter out all parameters that they interpret on their own (for example,* "`-nograp`"*, which is an option useful for debugging KDE programs).*

7 *Actually, we should check this case a little bit more intensively, but the assumption is correct for almost all cases.*

`timeout()`, calling the slot `slotForcedLoad()`. The constructor of KTsp is already finished and `app->exec()` in `main()` is being executed. The Slot `slotForceLoad()` is trivial; it only passes the URL to `loadFile()`.

With this small construction, we guarantee that loading and optimization doesn't occur in the constructor and that the "event loop" of Qt is started in `app->exec()` before. We haven't restricted ourselves to local files. If you have a `kdelnk` file for KTsp on your desktop, you can point kfm to an FTP server, drag a TSP out of it, and drop it on the corresponding icon.

7

Session Management

Before we can finish the pure programming part of KTsp, we need one more integral property. Open a document with KWrite and log out of KDE. When you restart KDE, KWrite will be on the correct desktop with the opened document. This feature is called Session Management. It means that an application "memorizes" its internal state at the end of a session and later restores it at the next session.

Naturally, "memorizes" means saving the corresponding data to a file that will be read at the beginning of the next session. In our case, it's `$HOME/.kde/share/config/ktsprc.1`. Most of it is done by KDE—the desktop where KTsp has been, the size of the window, the position of the menubar and toolbar...everything will be saved without a single line of code from the programmer. However, KDE doesn't know anything about the data being edited by our program. We have to take care of saving it ourselves.

7.1 KTsp Memorizes the TSP

This data is the TSP being processed by KTsp. During the first try, we will see if we can get KTsp to load and process the same TSP. A naive approach would be to just memorize the filename or the URL. A drawback to this approach is that the file could have been deleted between the sessions or that the remote computer isn't online to provide the URL. It's better to save the data in a temporary file and to delete it later when KTsp is automatically started in the next session.

To make the Session Management possible, we have to change `main()` a little bit:

```
int main( int argc, char* argv[] )
  {
  KApplication app( argc, argv );
  if ( app.isRestored() )
    {
    RESTORE( KTsp );
```

```
    }
  else
    {
    QString s = "";
    if ( argc > 1 )
      {
      KURL *url = new KURL( argv[1] );
      CHECK_PTR( url );
      if ( url->isMalformed() )
        {
        s = QDir::currentDirPath();
        s += "/";
        }
      s += argv[1];
      delete url;
      }
    KTsp *ktsp = new KTsp( s );
    CHECK_PTR( ktsp );
    ktsp->show();
    }
  return app.exec();
  }
```

After creating the instance of KApplication, we use `KApplication::isRestored()` to check whether KTsp has been started because of Session Managment. In this case, we're provided with the macro `RESTORE()` from KApplication, which handles restoring the KTMW. The argument being passed to the macro is the class name of the KTMW that is supposed to be restored, not the name of the program. We can always use `RESTORE()` when only one kind of KTMW has to be restored.[1] Everything is restored except those things that relate to the TSP itself. The main window appears at the correct place and in the right size. The menubar and toolbar are just like they were before leaving KDE.

Now, we have to take care of the actual data. The virtual methods `saveProperties()` and `readProperties()` are provided by KTMW for this reason. We just overwrite them. Let's start with `saveProperties()`:

```
void KTsp::saveProperties( KConfig *config )
  {
  if ( _numberOfPoints != 0 )
    {
    QString s = tmpnam( 0 );
    if( tsp->saveTsp( s, ORIG_TSP ) )
      {
      config->writeEntry( "Points", _numberOfPoints ),
      config->writeEntry( "Neighbours", tsp->numberOfNeighbours() );
```

[1] *Actually, we have two different kinds of KTMWs, KTsp and View, but we ignore View and restore only KTsp.*

```
        config->writeEntry( "Runs", _runs );
        config->writeEntry( "OrigName", s );
        }
      }
    }
```

We will do something only if a TSP has already been loaded or created, which means the number of points is not equal to 0. The C function `tmpnam()` provides a filename for a temporary file guaranteeing that it's a unique name in the whole system. Next, we let `TspGda::saveTsp()` save the original TSP in this file. If it hasn't worked, we won't do anything else. KTsp will be started at the beginning of the next session, but without an opened TSP.

The next lines pass important values, including the name of the temporary file, to KConfig. We use the exact same mechanism as for saving the configuration of our program. However, we don't set a group; KTMW has taken care of it for us. We have to modify `TspGda::saveTsp()` a little bit so that it saves the correct TSP. The changes are trivial:

```
bool TspGda::saveTsp( QString name, int which )
  {
  Point *p = 0;
  switch ( which )
    {
    case KTsp::ORIG_TSP:
      p = points;
      break;
    case KTsp::CURRENT_TSP:
      p = actualPoints;
      break;
    case KTsp::BEST_TSP:
      p = bestPoints;
      break;
    }
  emit statusChanged( KTsp::STATUSBAR_SAVING );
  if ( !io->saveTsp( name, p, _numberOfPoints ) )
    {
    emit statusChanged( KTsp::STATUSBAR_SAVE_ERROR );
    return false;
    }
  else
    {
    emit statusChanged( KTsp::STATUSBAR_READY );
    return true;
    }
  }
```

In addition to the filename, we pass the ID of the correct TSP to the method, which will be chosen in the *switch* statement. These are all the changes needed to save the current session. The restoration at the beginning of the next one has to be analyzed. First, `KTsp::readProperties()` is as follows:

```
void KTsp::readProperties( KConfig *config )
  {
  int points;
  int neighbours;
  int runs;
  points = config->readNumEntry( "Points", 0 );
  neighbours = config->readNumEntry( "Neighbours", 0 );
  runs = config->readNumEntry( "Runs", 0 );
  if ( runs == 0 ) runs = _runs;
  QString s = config->readEntry( "OrigName" );
  if ( ( points >= 10 ) &&
       ( ( neighbours >= 3 ) && ( neighbours < points ) ) &&
       ( !s.isEmpty() ) )
    {
    tsp->setNumberOfNeighbours( neighbours );
    _runs = runs;
    resumedTsp = s;
    timer = new QTimer( this, "Resume Timer" );
    CHECK_PTR( timer );
    connect( timer, SIGNAL( timeout() ),
             this, SLOT( slotForcedResume() ) );
    timer->start( 500, true );
    }
  else
    {
    // data inconsistent
    // let's try to remove the temporary file
    QFile f( s );
    f.remove();
    }
  }
```

Just as the last time, reading the information is more complicated than writing it. First we have to read the previously saved values. In the *if* statement, we check them because it is possible that someone has edited the file. If any inconsistencies appear, we will try only to delete the file. KTsp would be restored without a TSP.

If the data looks okay, it will be saved in the program. Now, we face a similar dilemma to one we've already faced with the command line. If we pass the filename within `readProperties()` to `TspGda`, the optimization will start before `KApplication:exec()` is called. In this special case, `KTMW::show()` won't even be called. Because that isn't acceptable at all, we'll use the same trick as with the filename in the command line. The name of the temporary file is already saved in a member variable of KTsp. We create an instance of

QTimer and connect its signal `timeout()` with the slot `KTsp::slotForcedResume()`:

```
void KTsp::slotForcedResume()
  {
  disableOpenNew();
  tsp->resumeTsp( resumedTsp, _runs );
  enableOpenNew();
  }
```

When the time expires (and `KTMW::show()`, just as `KApplication::exec()`, has been called), the program control will continue in this slot. Just like every time we load a TSP, we block all menu items and toolbar items related to loading and generating. Next, we let `TspGda::resumeTsp()` load the temporary file and reactivate loading and generating of TSPs. Let's consider `resumeTsp()`:

```
void TspGda::resumeTsp( QString name, int iterations )
  {
  startTsp( name, iterations, RESUME_TSP );
  }

void TspGda::startTsp( QString name, int iterations, int mode )
  {
  stopped = false;

  switch( mode )
    {
    case GENERATE_TSP:
      checkOldTsp();
      emit statusChanged( KTsp::STATUSBAR_GENERATING );
      points = io->generateTsp( _confNumberOfPoints, _confNumberOfNeighbours );
      break;

    case LOAD_TSP:
      {
      emit statusChanged( KTsp::STATUSBAR_LOADING );
      kapp->processEvents();
      Point *pTemp = io->loadTsp( name, _confNumberOfNeighbours );
      if ( pTemp == 0 )
        {
        emit statusChanged( KTsp::STATUSBAR_LOAD_ERROR );
        return;
        }
      checkOldTsp();
      points = pTemp;
      }
      break;

    case RESUME_TSP:
      {
      emit statusChanged( KTsp::STATUSBAR_RESUMING );
      kapp->processEvents();
```

```
        Point *pTemp = io->loadTsp( name, _numberOfNeighbours, true );
        if ( pTemp == 0 )
          {
          emit statusChanged( KTsp::STATUSBAR_RESUME_ERROR );
          return;
          }
        checkOldTsp();
        points = pTemp;
        }
        break;
      }
```

TspGda::resumeTsp() passes the task through to startTsp() with the corresponding parameters. There, we've changed the *if* statement through a *switch* statement that distinguishes between generating, normal loading, and loading by Session Management. This branch of Session Management differs from the one for normal loading only through the signal being sent to the GUI and through the additional argument "true" for TspIO::loadTsp(). The rest of the method hasn't changed. TspIO will show us what the "true" is supposed to be:

```
Point *loadTsp( QString name, int neighbours = 10,
                bool remove = false );
```

We expanded the declaration of Tsp10::loadTsp() with bool parameter, remove preset to false. It informs the method whether the file from which the TSP is loaded shall be removed afterwards. The preset value makes sure that this won't happen for normal loading. Accordingly, calling this method for normal loading hasn't changed. In the case of loading as a consequence of Session Management, however, we actually want the file to be deleted right after it has been read. The only change in the implementation of TspIO::loadTsp() is a QFile::remove() right after a QFile::close().

7.2 KTsp Memorizes the Best Solution

If you have played around with the Session Management for a while, you have probably seen that it's not enough yet. All results of KTsp that were calculated before logging out are lost—among them possibly the best result ever. Instead, KTsp begins from the beginning on. We want to change that.

In addition to the best result so far, our program should remember how many runs it has already completed. The progress bar has to be restored correspondingly, as does the "All runs" display. It's not only supposed to work when KTsp has been terminated in the middle of everything, but even when optimization has not yet been started or is already finished.

Install ktsp-0.0.11 and test the Session Management. You'll see the program behaving as it's supposed to. We had to change KTsp::saveProperties()

and `KTsp::readProperties()` a little bit. First, let's take a look at the saving:

```
void KTsp::saveProperties( KConfig *config )
  {
  if ( _numberOfPoints != 0 )
    {
    QString s1 = tmpnam( 0 );
    QString s2 = tmpnam( 0 );
    bool orig = tsp->saveTsp( s1, ORIG_TSP );
    bool best = tsp->saveTsp( s2, BEST_TSP );
    if( orig && best )
      {
      config->writeEntry( "Points", _numberOfPoints ),
      config->writeEntry( "Neighbours", tsp->numberOfNeighbours() );
      config->writeEntry( "Runs", _runs );
      config->writeEntry( "CurrentRun", progressBar->progress() );
      QString s;
      s.setNum( bestQuality, 'g', 60 );
      config->writeEntry( "BestQuality", s );
      config->writeEntry( "OrigName", s1 );
      config->writeEntry( "BestName", s2 );
      s = "";
      int n = rDisplay->numberOfValues();
      if ( n > 0 )
        {
        s.setNum( rDisplay->firstValue(), 'g', 60 );
        s += "\n";
        QString tmp;
        for ( int i = 1; i < n; i++ )
          {
          tmp.setNum( rDisplay->nextValue(), 'g', 60 );
          s += tmp + "\n";
          }
        config->writeEntry( "ReceivedValues", s );
        }
      }
    else
      {
      QFile f( s1 );
      f.remove();
      f.setName( s2 );
      f.remove();
      }
    }
  }
```

Because KTsp is now supposed to memorize the original TSP as well as the current best optimized one, the best one has to be saved in a temporary file, too. In case the saving has succeeded, we write all the relevant data with `KConfig::writeEntry()`. Additionally, we save the number of runs completed so far and the name of the temporary file with the optimized TSP. We also need the quality of the best TSP so that `TspGda` has a comparison value that it can use to decide if the following TSPs are better. We don't write the quality directly with `writeEntry()` because the preset precision isn't enough. Instead, we convert the value with the highest precision possible to a QString and write this one.

We demanded the display "All runs" to be restored completely, so we must save all the values displayed by it. There aren't many. We can just write them in the configuration file of Session Management instead of writing them to another temporary file. The *if* statement, along with the following *for* loop, handles it. One after another, we read the values from the instance of `RunsDisplay` and write them in a QString divided by a Newline "\n". The whole string is saved with `writeEntry()`.

If we fail to create one or both of the temporary files (the original and the best TSP) at the beginning, we'll try to remove at the end what has been created so as to keep the system clean.

Now, let's take a look at `KTsp::readProperties()`:

```
void KTsp::readProperties( KConfig *config )
  {
  int points;
  int neighbours;
  int runs;
  points = config->readNumEntry( "Points", 0 );
  neighbours = config->readNumEntry( "Neighbours", 0 );
  runs = config->readNumEntry( "Runs", 0 );
  if ( runs == 0 ) runs = _runs;
  QString s1 = config->readEntry( "OrigName" );
  QString s2 = config->readEntry( "BestName" );
  if ( ( points >= 10 ) &&
       ( ( neighbours >= 3 ) && ( neighbours < points ) ) &&
       ( !s1.isEmpty() ) &&
       ( !s2.isEmpty() ) )
    {
    tsp->setNumberOfNeighbours( neighbours );
    _runs = runs;
    resumedOrigTsp = s1;
    resumedBestTsp = s2;
    QString s = config->readEntry( "ReceivedValues" );
    rDisplay->slotClearDisplay();
    rDisplay->slotNumberOfRuns( runs );
    resumedBestQuality = config->readDoubleNumEntry( "BestQuality" );
    performedRuns = config->readNumEntry( "CurrentRun", 0 );
    if ( !s.isEmpty() )
      {
      QTextStream t( s, IO_ReadOnly );
      QString tmp;
      while ( !t.eof() )
        {
        tmp = t.readLine();
        rDisplay->slotNextValue( tmp.toDouble() );
        }
```

```
    }
  timer = new QTimer( this, "Resume Timer" );
  CHECK_PTR( timer );
  connect( timer, SIGNAL( timeout() ),
           this, SLOT( slotForcedResume() ) );
  timer->start( 500, true );
  }
else
  {
  // data inconsistent
  // let's try to remove the temporary files
  QFile f( s1 );
  f.remove();
  f.setName( s2 );
  f.remove();
  }
}
```

That's where we read all the data and pass it either directly to the corresponding classes or save it for use in the slot `slotForceResume()`. It's probably a surprise that a QString with a `QTextStream` can be used just like a file. In the *while* loop, we read the data for the display "All runs" from the QString and pass it to the display. Finally, we use a QTimer again to delay the start of the optimization until `KApplication::exec()` has been called:

```
void KTsp::slotForcedResume()
  {
  disableOpenNew();
  noClearDisplay = true;
  tsp->resumeTsp( resumedOrigTsp, resumedBestTsp,
                  _runs, performedRuns,
                  resumedBestQuality );
  enableOpenNew();
  }
```

`KTsp::slotForceResume()` hasn't changed much. We pass some more arguments needed for the new tasks to `TspGda::resumeTsp()`. The corresponding changes in `TspGda` are more or less trivial. In addition, we set the flag `noClearDisplay` to true. This is necessary because we've already created the display "All runs" at this time and have to prevent it from being deleted. The corresponding code in `KTsp::slotStatusChanged()` looks like this:

```
case STATUSBAR_OPTIMIZING:
   delete progress;
   if ( !noClearDisplay )
     {
     rDisplay->slotClearDisplay();
     rDisplay->slotNumberOfRuns( _runs );
     }
   noClearDisplay = false;
   aDisplay->slotClearDisplay();
   statusBar()->changeItem( i18n( "Optimizing" ), 0 );
   break;
```

The display "All runs" is deleted only if KTsp has been started in Normal mode and not via Session Management.

Our program KTsp is finished; we're at the end of the programming. Naturally, there is always more that can be done. For example, KTsp optimizes the way that the hypothetical drilling machine has to move, but that's not what our workshop manager really wants. He's interested in how long the treatment of the work piece takes. Because the drilling head does not move in a uniform way from one hole to the other—but speeds up and slows down—the time it needs is not proportional to the distance moved. Actually, we would have to optimize the time needed instead of the distance moved. For this, we would have to change the methods `TspGda::nextAction()` and `TspGda::calcQuality()` and create a new possibility of configuring the properties of the drilling machine (acceleration, slowing down, and top speed) in KTsp. These things relate only to the precision with which the quality is being calculated, and have nothing to do with KDE programming. That's why we ignore this complex option and leave it to the one who wants to use the program in reality.

We might also create a possibility to actually watch the algorithm optimizing a TSP. This could be a display continuously adapted to the ongoing optimizations. Such a display would reduce the speed of the optimization significantly and wouldn't really be of much practical use. Because the required changes to implement such behavior would be real KDE programming, the reader might consider doing them as an exercise.

8 Localization

For a program to gain universal acceptance, it's not enough to just write the source code and "kill" the bugs. Users, as the word implies, must be able to *use* the program; and further, they must feel "at home" with it. KDE helps meet those conditions in a big way. It provides the programmer with a base framework from which to create easy-to-use and consistent environments.

KDE provides a significant advantage over the confusing number of different GUIs in X. Users who have learned to operate a KDE program won't have a problem with other programs either. Something important is still missing, however. KTsp enforces English as the language. Generally, this is a good compromise. Sometimes, however, it isn't so good. Consider, for example, a program such as a word processor that is supposed to have wide recognition. Consider further a Brazilian secretary who would have to learn all the relevant English words to effectively use the word processor (font type, font size, and so on). I don't think she would really appreciate it. And what about the Egyptian musician who wants to use the KDE score editor? English is probably not one of his strengths either.

The program will make the user feel "at home" only if it's supporting his native language. That's why one of the first goals of KDE was to support as many languages as possible. We want to use this property for KTsp.

8.1 KDE Supports More Than 30 Languages

At the printing of this book, KDE supported more than 30 languages, including exotic ones such as Bretonic and hard ones such as a simplified Chinese. The internationalization was based on this ideal: Users who neither want to read the source code nor compile it after the translation should be able to translate KDE to their native language.

This goal specified that internationalization (preparing for translations) and localization (the actual translation) must be strictly divided. We have already taken care of the internationalization in KTsp twice. First, we enclosed all strings with `i18n()`. This macro will not only make sure that all output appears in the correct language when the translations are available, it also will help us extract all strings from the source code. Second, we prepared all the widgets for different-sized texts by using layout managers. The last step for the internationalization was to extract the texts from the source code.

This part, the internationalization, has to be done by the programmer. There's only one thing left to do; he has to find a translator. The program—it doesn't matter whether in source or binary format—will be released with the extracted texts. The user can provide the translations (in other words, the localization).

This method has a significant advantage over other methods. The Icelandic Ministry of Education, for example, demands that all software in schools be available in Icelandic. A well-known software company refuses to provide the translations because the market is too small to generate a profit. Because of this decision, local KDE users began to translate KDE. The KDE internationalization model makes it possible for small groups to translate software into their native language as long as users are willing to do so.

8.2 The Translation

The two most important tools we will use are the programs `xgettext` and `msgfmt`. First, we need the file with all the extracted texts. Let's change into the directory of our source (`ktsp-0.1.0/ktsp`) and enter the following command:

```
xgettext -a -C -ki18n -s -d ktsp *.C
```

The options are as follows:

-a	All texts.
-C	Recognize C++ comments.
-k	The expression `i18n` specifies the beginning of a text.
-s	Sort the texts and delete copies.
-d	Name the result `ktsp.po`.

At the end, `*.C` instructs `xgettext` to search all files with the ending C for texts. After doing so, we get a file that looks like this:

```
#: ktsp.C:181
msgid "&Graphic Preferences..."
msgstr ""
```

```
#: ktsp.C:119
msgid "&New TSP"
msgstr ""

#: ktsp.C:126
msgid "&Save as..."
msgstr ""
```

We will get a line with `msgid` and the text as a string for every text found. A second line begins with `msgstr` and contains an empty string. The empty string will later contain the translation (in our case, German).

We move the file `ktsp-0.1.0/ktsp/ktsp.po` to `ktsp-0.1.0/po/ktsp.pot`.[1] It will serve as the template for other translations. Now before we start deleting a lot of items, it's important to consider what we can keep and what we should ditch. Nearly all KDE programs have a menu called File. It doesn't make sense to translate this expression again for every program. You can find the file `kde.pot` in the source of the KDE libraries (kdelibs). Every text included in it can be deleted from `ktsp.pot`, if it means the same in your program.[2] KDE is intelligent enough to find the correct translation nonetheless. When we finish this exercise, we'll get our real template.

We'll copy it from `ktsp-0.1.0/ktsp/ktsp.po` to `ktsp-0.1.0/po/ktsp.pot` and start with the translations. The following represents a small part from `de.po` that has already been translated:

```
#: ktsp.C:392
msgid "Generating neighbours"
msgstr "Nachbarn erzeugen"

#: ktsp.C:445
msgid "For point: %d"
msgstr "F_r Punkt: %d"

#: ktsp.C:190
msgid ""

"KTsp - The TSP Optimizer\n"
"Version 0.1.0\n"
"\n"
"(c) 1999 Uwe Thiem\n"
"uwe@kde.org\n"
"\n"
"The algorithm GDA has\n"
"been invented by\n"
"Gunter Dueck."
```

[1] *Please remember to rename* `ktsp.po` *to* `ktsp.pot`. *The t stands for template.*

[2] *This is not always the case. Think, for example, of an English verb and its substantive forms looking the same from time to time. This differs, however, in the German translation. Think of words such as close, which can mean schliessen as well as nah or dicht.*

```
msgstr ""
"KTsp - Der TSP Optimierer\n"
"Version 0.1.0\n"
"\n"
" (c) 1999 Uwe Thiem\n"
"uwe@kde.org\n"
"\n"
"Der Algorithmus GDA wurde\n"
"von Gunter Dueck \n"
"entwickelt."
```

The first example is normal text in a single line. After `msgstr`, we just enter the German expression. The second example shows that translated texts can look like format strings in C. In the example, `%d` will be replaced by a value. The third example is more complicated. It's a multiline text that will be shown in the About box in the Help menu. First, it's remarkable that `xgettext` extracted the whole text even though it had multiple lines. We translate the item line for line, but the translation doesn't have to contain as many lines as the original one. By the way, the translator can skip whole messages if he can't come up with a translation right now. They'll be shown in the original language.

After we've translated the texts into German, we must create a database from the file (which KDE must understand). The following command takes care of it:

```
msgfmt -o de.gmo -v de.po
```

The program `msgfmt` is intelligent enough to warn the user about small inconsistencies. It'll detect whether there's a Newline "\n" missing at the end when there's one in the original. We leave the resulting database `de.gmo` in the directory `ktsp/po`. The command "make install" will automatically install it in the right place in your system.

Here's a summary of what happens at runtime of the program: First, `i18n()` searches in the program-specific database for a translation. If it finds one, it uses it. If it can't find any, it searches in the KDE-wide database. If it doesn't find it there either, it uses the original (English) text. This approach has the following consequences:

- It'll never happen that no text appears onscreen. If no translation has been found, the original text displays.
- Translations in the program-specific database overwrite the ones in the KDE-wide database. If the program-wide database translates *Directory* as *Ordner*, and the program-specific database translates it as *Verzeichnis*, the final translation will be *Verzeichnis*.

- If a KDE-wide translation fits in the context of the program, you shouldn't provide your own translation (otherwise, you might confuse the user). The consistency of all KDE programs is more important than originality.

If the program is being expanded with new text later, the program "tupdate" will help to insert the new text into the already translated ones so that no translations are lost:

```
tupdate new.po old.po > latest.po
```

This command creates the file `latest.po`, which contains all the old and new translations.

Now install ktsp-0.1.0.tgz and switch KDE to (German). Besides seeing KTsp presented in German, you can also take a look at the layout management, which we've implemented with all this hard work, in action. All elements adjust their size to the text.

8.3 And How Do I Get a Finnish Translation?

If you're a language genius, you'll be able to do it just like the German translation. Copy `ktsp.pot` to `fi.po`, translate the text, and create the database of the Finnish translations:

```
msgfmt -o fi.gmo -v fi.po
```

If you can do this, congratulations and applause. Most programmers, however, really aren't language geniuses and we haven't strictly divided internationalization and localization for the fun of it. It is better to let the Finnish do the translation for us.

The KDE Web server contains the page `www.kde.org/i18n.html`, which contains all the information that relates to "translations." The information in Figure 8.1 might be outdated when you read this book, but the original page of the KDE server will always provide you with new information. You should read the original page before you contact the corresponding persons because they could have changed.

Strictly speaking, this process is pretty easy. If you write a freeware program and the program is in a state where the text won't change that often anymore, create a `*.pot` file of our program. Now send an email to the coordinator of KDE Internationalization and ask him to add your program to the project. He'll contact you and ask you to send him the `*.pot` file. If special expressions need more explanation (perhaps the translator doesn't know the translation corresponding to the context of your program), you'll have to provide them.

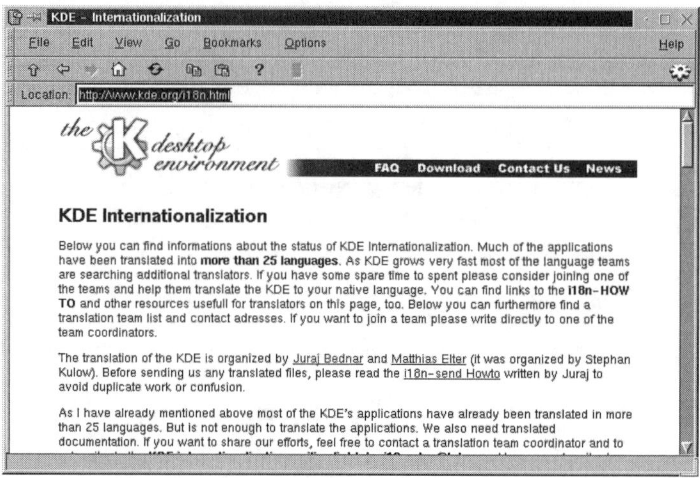

Figure 8.1 *KDE's Web site that relates to "translations."*

From this moment on, the whole thing is in the hands of the translators. Please bear in mind that everyone works on this voluntarily (without demanding money for it), just like the KDE programmers. Remember, also, that the translators actually have other lives as students and employees (besides this work as KDE translators). Putting pressure on them will only lead to your project sliding down the priority list. On the other hand, a few friendly words never go amiss.

If you write a commercial program, which can be Open Source, too,[3] there're many ways to get a translation. Naturally, you can hire professional translators. You can also contact the KDE translation team and make a freelance translation offer. Of course, a donation to KDE might help to find translators, too (if not, it will certainly endear you to the community). In every case, please remember that the KDE angels are all people working on this for nothing in their spare time.

[3] *Confusion seems to follow the expressions Open Source, commercial software, and proprietary software. Commercial software is something that can be sold. This can also be Open Source if the source code is released and if you pay attention to certain rules. The Trolls's Qt library is a good example of this. Proprietary software does not make its source code available. Most commercial software (but not all) is proprietary, too.*

9 Documentation

All KDE programs open a window with Help text when you click on Help, Contents (or press F1). Most programs provide a Help index with clickable entries. These Help texts are HTML documents shown by dkehelp, a small browser functioning as the Help viewer. Users who display KTsp Help will see only the text "Yet to be written." Of course, we want a nice little online handbook for KTsp, too.

9.1 The Online Help for KTsp

Because KDE Help consists of nothing more than HTML files, those files can be generated with every HTML editor (or even with vi). If you have some artistic talent, you'll probably think about adding graphics and elaborated HTML documents. It might look great, but please remember that KDE is all about consistency. Users not only want to be able to control the program, but also to easily navigate in Help. That's why every KDE program should have a similar Help system.

Luckily, KDE provides a lot of tools to help us with this. Therefore, we won't just get a Help system that looks similar to ones in other KDE programs, but one that also is formatted nicely. And importantly, we don't have to be artists to create such a Help system.[1] We don't generate HTML directly; instead, we take the detour over SGML, which you can easily convert to HTML, and also to PS documents, in case you want to provide printed handbooks for your program. First, it's important to mention a few tools that can help us but that are not part of the official distribution of KDE:

- **KlyX**—This is a graphical front end for the famous typesetting system TeX/LaTeX. For most of us, LaTeX is a closed book because of its

[1] *An artist? That's something that I definitely am not. I always got negative credits for my drawings with a ruler and a pair of compasses in math class.*

cryptic syntax. KlyX takes care of the syntax for you. If it's not provided by your Linux distribution, you can either get it from the KDE FTP server at `ftp:://ftp.kde.org/pub/kde` or you can install LyX (which provides the same features, but not such a "comfortable" interface). If you create larger documents frequently, you should install KlyX anyway.

- **TeX/LaTeX**—Because KlyX and LyX are front ends for TeX/LaTeX, you'll need them, too. To my knowledge, there's no Linux distribution that doesn't provide TeX/LaTeX. Just take a look at your handbooks and install the corresponding package if you haven't done so already.
- **kdesdk**—This KDE Software Development Kit is a collection of useful tools. You can download it from the KDE FTP server at `ftp://ftp.kde.org/pub/kde`. For this discussion, we're interested in ksgml2html, which is a part of kdesdk. Please install it in the usual way.

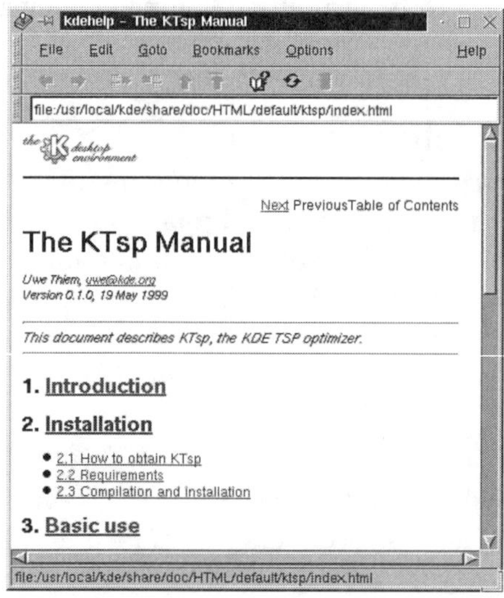

Figure 9.1 *The KTsp handbook...*

Open a new document with KlyX (or LyX) without a template and with the name index.lyx. You can use another name, but it will complicate the process later on down the line. For the layout in KlyX, you select Layout, Document, Class, SGML. Now, write your handbook in KlyX. Normally, I wouldn't distribute the LyX file of a handbook, but I did it in this case to give you a template for your own handbook. You'll find the file in `ktsp-0.1.0/ktsp/doc/en/index.lyx`. After you have finished your handbook, export it by selecting File, Export, LinuxDoc, and assign the name `index.sgml`. Now, complete the final step to create the HTML files, as follows:

```
ksgml2html index.sgml en
```

This command generates all the files needed for the online manual, which will look similar to the one shown in Figure 9.1. The command-line parameter `en` specifies the language of the document and is internally used by ksmgl2html. After calling it, two questions appear. The first one asks you to give a short description of your handbook. I used "The KDE TSP Optimizer" in this case. The second one asks for keywords. I answered with "KTsp KDE UNIX Linux TSP." As long as the generated HTML files aren't used on a Web server, but only online for your program, you don't have to care about the keywords. They're inserted in the META tag of the HTML header. Search machines on the Web can analyze the header and group the sites.

After you install ktsp-0.2.0, you can take a look at the handbook that I managed to create (without any artistic talent whatsoever).

9.2 Multilingual Online Help

Naturally, our users should have the handbook in their own language. Just as with the other texts in the program, we will use German as the example. We create the directory `ktsp-0.2.0/ktsp/doc/de`. We copy `index.lyx` and `logotp3.gif` to it. After we have translated the LyX file, we just repeat the whole procedure that we used for the English documentation. The following lines install them at the right places in the system:

```
ksgml2html index.sgml de
creates the HTML files and
make install
installs them at the right place on your system.
```

For every language the documentation is translated to, just repeat these steps. The actual problem is not to create the HTML files from the LyX file or to install them, but to get the translations. The team of KDE translators can help just as with the texts.

The German handbook is included with ktsp-0.2.0. You can see it in Figure 9.2.

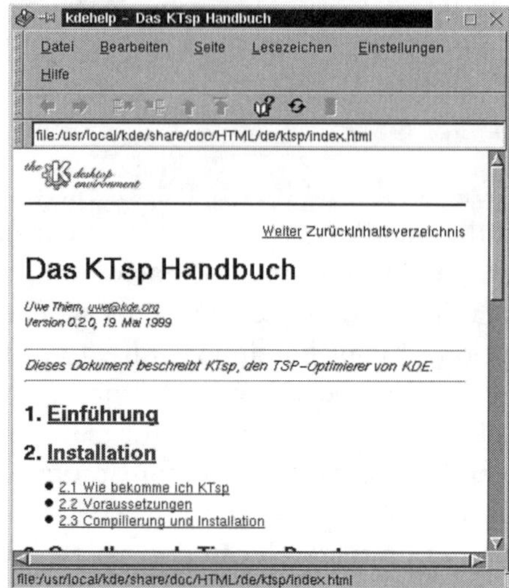

Figure 9.2 *...and the German handbook.*

10

Automated Make Process

As a developer, you have probably written a whole lot of non-trivial programs. You're familiar with make and Makefiles. Perhaps, you have wondered why Makefiles are always so big in KDE, whereas you normally get along with 30 or maybe 50 lines. This chapter discusses why KDE's Makefiles are so big, and how you can get to an automatic build process without a lot of work.

10.1 KDE Doesn't Just Run on Linux

The fact that KDE doesn't just run on Linux is the most important reason why the KDE Makefiles are so complicated. Even Linux doesn't always equal Linux. For example, many of the socket functions of Linux/Alpha are declared differently from those in Linux/Intel. And besides those, KDE also runs on FreeBSD, Solaris, and HPUX. Users have even got it to work on IRIX, True64 (formerly Digital UNIX), and other UNIX variants.

In addition, several X servers exist. Alone under Linux, three different standard X variants exist: XFree86, AcceleratedX, and Metro-X; and all support the X protocol, but still have small differences. On commercial UNIX variants, there are the proprietary X servers of the UNIX vendors. Normally, Qt hides all these small things from the application developer, but some programs have to work very close together with the X server (for example, screen savers).

Put simply, KDE has to be portable. If you've ever written programs for a bunch of UNIX variants using more than `cin`, `cout` and `cerr`, you'll know how fast Makefiles grow with the number of supported platforms and how fast the source gets confusing with all the `#ifdef`. KDE tries to go around these difficulties by using `autoconf` and `automake`.

You start every installation of a new version of KTsp with this line:

```
./configure
```

This command analyzes the system in depth. That's why it runs for a relatively long time, depending on the performance of your computer. It doesn't just guess: "Aha, we're on a FreeBSD system, so..."; it really checks for special headers, the parameters needed by some functions, whether there are special libraries installed on the system, and which functionality is provided. It compiles little programs and checks them for errors.

After it retrieves all the information, it generates the Makefiles in each directory of the project from the `Makefile.in` files. The Makefile will be used by "make." In addition, it creates a file named `config.h` in the main directory, which should be included via `#include`, by all source file programs that might need specific system knowledge.

Instead of writing Makefiles, we write `Makefile.in`. However, even `Makefile.in` tends to be long and complicated. That's why we use another tool to automatically create `Makefile.in`.

10.2 automake

automake takes care of this task. It generates `Makefile.in` from the `Makefile.am`. With `Makefile.am` we're finally where we wanted to be. It is really simple. Take a look at ktsp-0.2.0/Makefile.am:

```
# This file you have to edit. Change the name here
SUBDIRS = ktsp po

# not a GNU package. You can remove this line, if
# have all needed files, that a GNU package needs
AUTOMAKE_OPTIONS = foreign
```

It has only two items. The first one specifies the subdirectories of `ktsp-0.2.0`. The second one states that although it's licensed under the GPL,[1] it's still not a real GNU package and doesn't need all the Free Software Foundation (FSF) files. That's all. automake generates the 412-lines-big `Makefile.in` file out of it.

The file `ktsp-0.2.0/ktsp/Makefile.am` is somewhat more complicated, but still easy compared to Makefiles for portable programs:

```
# these 10 paths are KDE specific. Use them:
# kde_htmldir       Where your docs should go to. (contains lang subdirs)
# kde_appsdir       Where your application file (.kdelnk) should go to.
# kde_icondir       Where your icon should go to.
# kde_sounddir      Where system sounds should go to.
# kde_datadir       Where you install application data. (Use a subdir)
# kde_locale        Where translation files should go to.(contains lang subdirs)
```

[1] *You can find the GPL on the New Riders website.*

```
# kde_cgidir        Where cgi-bin executables should go to.
# kde_confdir       Where config files should go to.
# kde_mimedir       Where mimetypes should go to.
# kde_toolbardir    Where general toolbar icons should go to.
# kde_wallpaperdir  Where general wallpapers should go to.

# set the include path for X, qt and KDE
INCLUDES= $(all_includes)

# claim, which subdirectories you want to install
# if you don't have subdirectories, comment it
SUBDIRS = doc

####### This part is very ktsp specific
# you can add here more. This one gets installed
bin_PROGRAMS =  ktsp

# Which sources should be compiled for ktsp.
ktsp_SOURCES = main.cpp ktsp.C gda.C point.C random.C tspgda.C tspio.C
view.C canvas.C tspdialog.C graphicdialog.C graph.C graphdisplay.C
actionsdisplay.C runsdisplay.C

ktsp_METASOURCES =  USE_AUTOMOC

# the library search path.
ktsp_LDFLAGS = $(all_libraries) $(KDE_RPATH)

# the libraries to link against. Be aware of the order. First the libraries,
# that depend on the following ones.
ktsp_LDADD   = $(LIB_KFILE)

# this option you can leave out. Just, if you use "make dist", you
need it
noinst_HEADERS = ktsp.h gda.h point.h random.h tspgda.h tspio.h view.h
canvas.h tspdialog.h graphicdialog.h graph.h graphdisplay.h actionsdisplay.h
runsdisplay.h

# if you "make distclean", these files get removed. If you want to remove
# them while "make clean", use CLEANFILES
DISTCLEANFILES = $(ktsp_METASOURCES)

# make messages.po. Move this one to ../po/ and "make merge" in po
# the -x is for skipping messages already translated in kdelibs
messages:
        $(XGETTEXT) -C -ki18n -x $(includedir)/kde.pot $(ktsp_SOURCES) && mv
messages.po ../po/ktsp.pot
kdelnkdir = $(kde_appsdir)/Applications
kdelnk_DATA = ktsp.kdelnk

icondir = $(kde_icondir)
icon_DATA = ktsp.xpm

# just install datas here. Use install-exec-local for scripts and etc.
```

```
# the binary itself is already installed from automake
# use mkinstalldirs, not "install -d"
# don't install a list of files. Just one file per install.
# if you have more of them, create a subdirectory with an extra Makefile
install-data-local:
	$(mkinstalldirs) $(kde_minidir)
	$(INSTALL_DATA) $(srcdir)/mini-ktsp.xpm $(kde_minidir)/ktsp.xpm
	$(INSTALL_DATA) $(srcdir)/run.xpm $(kde_toolbardir)/run.xpm

# remove ALL you have installed in install-data-local or install-exec-local
uninstall-local:
	-rm -f $(kde_minidir)/ktsp.xpm
```

The comment at the beginning informs us about the 10 symbolic names for the paths, which should be used instead of explicitly writing paths to Makefiles. Only because of this, is it possible for KDE to exist on different systems at different paths and the installation still work fine.

Most of the items are self-explanatory. Some are interesting enough for us to take a closer look at them. After we have specified the subdirectories, the program name, and the source files that have to be compiled, we get to this line:

```
ktsp_METASOURCES =  USE_AUTOMOC
```

This line relates to the Qt Metacompiler (`moc`).

A source file has to be created by `moc` from all the header files that contain `Q_OBJECT`. It can be compiled just like any other file. At the beginning of the book, I talked about the line

```
moc -o mysource.moc.cpp mysource.h
```

creating the source file from the header file. If we want to automate this process, we can't just insert the `*.moc.cpp` files into the source files in `Makefile.am`; they don't exist at the beginning. The tool `automoc` helps us. It's a Perl script searching all header files for `Q_OBJECT` and inserting the corresponding items to the METASOURCES in `Makefile.in`.

The program itself, the icon for the program, and the `ktsp.kdelnk`[2] file will be automatically installed by `make install`. Additionally, we want to install a mini icon (for example, in the menu of KPanel and in the title bar of the KTsp windows) and an icon for our toolbar. The last lines in `Makefile.am` serve this purpose.

Take a look at `Makefile.am` in the other subdirectories. They're all rather simple to understand. As long as you don't need another functionality for `automake/autoconf`, all changes in `Makefile.am` are very simple. It'll be enough

2 *I'll get back to this file later.*

in most cases. If you need other functions, it will be significantly harder—changes must be made in the files `acconfig.h` and/or `acinclude.m4`. The details of `automake`/`autoconf` are beyond the scope of this book. So, it's up to you to become an expert about it by yourself; or you can always ask for help on the KDE mailing lists.

10.3 A New Project

How can we start a completely new project? The simplest method is to use an existing project and to delete all sources, icons, translations, and so on. All references to the old project (including sources, icons, and so forth) in `Makefile.am` have to be replaced with references to your new project. All references must be replaced in the file `configure.in` in the main directory of your project, too. Search especially for `AC_OUTPUT` and adjust the directory structure to your project. Also determine whether the subdirectory `.deps` is deleted in the directory with the sources (in this case, `ktsp-0.2.0/ktsp`). If not, delete it. After you have finished this procedure and have created at least a source file with `main()`, enter the following sequence of commands:

```
autoconf
automake
perl automoc
./configure
make
```

All files will be updated. If you add new source files (or translations, icons, and so forth), you must adjust the file `Makefile.am` in the corresponding directory. Don't forget to begin the sequence with `automake` again. If you add new subdirectories, you have to adjust `configure.in` and begin with `autoconf`.

If your project has reached the state where you want to release it, you should delete all the compiled and linked files as well as core dumps and system-specific information created by `configure`. The following command takes care of it:

```
Make maintainer-clean
```

Next, your user has to enter only the three lines you are already familiar with from installing the different versions of KTsp:

```
./configure
make
make install
```

Now, what project should you start with? You can begin with KTsp. Actually, KDE is now evolving very quickly, as are `automake` and `autoconf`. In fact, this part of KTsp will probably already be outdated upon the release of this book. That's why it's a better choice to download and use a current project from `ftp.kde.org`.[3] The best course of action is to use a project that is similar to your own—not in what the program does, but how it is structured. Do you want to install your own library? Use a project doing the same thing. Is the source code of your project distributed over many subdirectories? Use a project that is also distributed over many subdirectories.

This should give you a good start. If you still encounter problems, the KDE mailing lists can probably help you.

10.4 Icons and Other Small Files

Besides source code, KDE projects have another bunch of important files for the GUI programs. You have already learned about the translation and the online Help. Icons are essential GUI elements that every program needs. There's the icon representing the program itself. We need it in two variants. The normal size, which is used on the desktop and on the panel; and a mini icon, which is used on the title bar of the program window, in the menus of the panel, and on the taskbar.

10.4.1 Icon and Mini Icon

Because you need an icon specific for your program, you'll have to do it on your own. KIconEdit, an excellent tool, can help you with this task. KIconEdit automatically takes care of the correct size and the correct color palette, because there are still a lot of 8-bit displays. The KDE icons are all drawn with the same color palette being displayed by KIconEdit right next to the drawing. It helps to leave enough colors for the application itself on the old displays.

If you don't think you can draw something representing your program adequately and looking somewhat aesthetic, you can contact the KDE artist team, which has developed most of the icons for KDE. You should give them a description of your program and maybe a sketch of the icon so that they can imagine how the program might best be represented. The coordinator of the team at the printing of this book is Torsten Rahn (`torsten@kde.org`).[4] Please remember that the artists are volunteers, too,

[3] *Attention! If your Linux distribution isn't up to date, you might need a new version of* `automake/autoconf`. *Take a look at the FTP server of your Linux distribution or ask your Linux distributor.*

[4] *Naturally, the KDE artists are happy to have others join them. If you have the skills and want to provide them to KDE, this is the right address for you.*

doing this work besides their regular activities as students, designers, and so on. The drawing of good icons is very difficult. So, you can imagine that the artists are very busy.

10.4.2 More Icons

Apart from the icon and the mini icon for the program itself, you'll need more icons for the toolbar. Luckily, they exist for most of the functions such as Open, Save, Print, Cut, Copy, Insert, and so forth. You need your own only if you insert a function that does not have an existing icon onto the toolbar. Basically, creating these icons works the same way as creating those we talked about in the preceding paragraph. Either you draw them yourself with KIconEdit or you ask the team of artists.

10.4.3 The File ktsp.kdelnk

A kdelnk file is assigned to every KDE program and contains a bunch of information about the program. The one for KTsp looks like the following:

```
# KDE Config File
[KDE Desktop Entry]
Type=Application
Protocols=file;ftp;
Exec=ktsp -caption "%c" %i %m %u
Icon=ktsp.xpm
MiniIcon=ktsp.xpm
DocPath=ktsp/index.html
Comment=The TSP Optimizer
Comment[de]=Der TSP Optimierer
Name=TSP Optimizer
Name[de]=TSP Optimierer
Terminal=0
MimeType=text/tsp
```

The first two lines characterize the file as one that can be placed on the desktop and can be clicked on. The third line specifies it as an application (and not a device such as a floppy drive or an URL). The protocols understood by the application are specified in the fourth line; in this case, local files (but also over NFS, because these files are treated like local ones) and FTP.

The next line specifies how the program is executed. First, the name of the program file `ktsp`. The next two parameters set the text in the title bar: `-caption` specifies that the following string is to be displayed in the title bar and `%c` means that the string doesn't stand directly in it, but has to be loaded from the `Name` line. In this case, `%c` will be set to the `TSP Optimierer` if we've set the language to German or to `TSP Optimizer` in all other cases because it's the standard item. The parameters `%i` and `%m` will be replaced by

`-icon ktsp.xpm`, and `-miniicon ktsp.xpm`, respectively; whereas the names of the icons correspond to the items `Icon` and `Miniicon`. That's how the icons can have a different name from the program itself.

Lines 6 and 7 specify the name of `Icon` and `MiniIcon`, whereas KDE looks in the right directories by itself. Line 8 tells KDE where the online Help of the program can be found. The directory structure of the online Help looks like this:

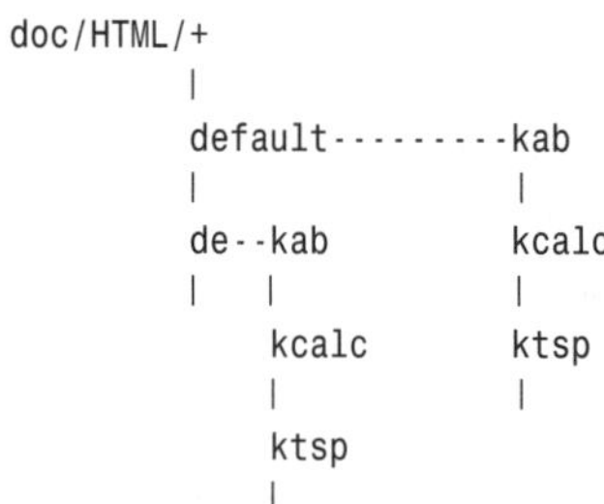

That's why it's enough to specify `ktsp/index.html` to find the correct file for all languages.

The "comment" lines contain the texts for the corresponding languages of the ToolTips of the program. It's the same with the `Name` lines, but they contain the name of the program displayed on the menus of the panels and on the desktop. The shortcut for the language displays right after "Comment" and "Name." The line `Terminal=0` specifies the program as a GUI application that doesn't need a terminal to run in.

Apart from the first two lines, the order of the items in the `*.kdelnk` file doesn't matter at all.

10.5 Install KTsp Correctly

After you have finished your new project, `make install` will have to install everything at the right place. There are a lot of symbols for the directories where KTsp should be installed available in the `Makefile.am`. They're all similar to `kde_appsdir`. To ensure that your files end up in the right places, you *x* use these symbols and not "hard" code the paths in the Makefiles.

Distributors install KDE in many ways. Some have the central KDE directory tree in `/opt` or `/usr/local`. Some spread KDE over `/usr/bin`, `/usr/lib`, and so on. If you make assumptions that the executable file of your program is under `$SOMETHING/kde/bin`, it'll probably be correct for your system: It might be totally false for another one, however. That's why you should use the predefined symbols in your `Makefile.am`. The command `./configure` with its several parameters will take care of converting these symbols to the correct paths.

11 Hints Regarding the Style

11.1 The Source Code

KDE is very liberal and doesn't have any rules about the style you have to use in your project. If you choose

```
foo( int something ) {
  blablabla;
}
```

or

```
foo( int something )
{
  blablabla;
}
```

or

```
foo( int something )
  {
  blablabla;
  }
```

or some other formatting, the style is totally left up to you as long as it can be read by people. It doesn't matter if you indent your source with spaces or tabs or whether you use two, four, or eight spaces; that's your call. It's your project and you have to feel at home in your source code to work on it productively. KDE is no monolith block where everyone has to do as the other ones. The goal is a consistent and uniform desktop for Linux and not a uniform source code.

It's different when you edit projects from others or libraries. To be polite, you should adapt to the style used there, even if you absolutely can't stand it.

11.2 Filename Extensions

We write our programs in C++, and we can use various extensions for it: .C, .cpp, .c++, .cc. It's up to you to choose one. I prefer .C—not least to show that we're on a UNIX system, which is case sensitive. Just a little hint if you're not a friend of cpp: `automoc` creates filenames such as `*.moc.cpp`. The whole mechanism of the Makefiles will work only if at least one of the source files has a .cpp extension. That's why I use `main.cpp` and name all my other files as `*.C`.

11.3 Comments

Some people (well, actually, many) think that there has to be "political correctness" in the source code. We at KDE don't care about that. Why shouldn't the developer be able to let his displeasure take its course

```
// shit! we are traversing a cursor on a deleted list
```

if only he and the other developers will see it. I just can't imagine why someone would have a problem with it; but I know that there are such people (or so I've heard). We write software, not Be Nice books.

11.4 Colours

We tend to look at colours as easily distinguishable. In general, that's true. The whole theory of false-colour photography is based on us being able to distinguish between colours more than between grayscales.

There's an anecdote from the beginning of KDE. The icons for "mounted" and "unmounted" floppy disks and CDs differed only through the use of a red and a green rectangle. It's obvious, isn't it? Actually, many people have a red-green faintness and can't distinguish the icons. Blue-green faintness is more rare, but many people can't distinguish those colours either. An even rarer person is the one who fits into the third category: persons who can't differentiate between any colours.

In summary, never make the visualization of differences in your program colour dependent only. We don't want to exclude all these colour-impaired people.

11.5 Icons and Graphics

Icons (in particular) and graphics (in general) are normally intuitive and self-explanatory. That's why they're often used for long descriptions. "A picture is worth a thousand words." Well, they are intuitive, but only in connection with the culture from which they came. Intuitive thinking is a synthetic act that isn't based on deduction. It works only if the picture really rings a bell in us. You won't believe me?

Let's take a look at the icon of KMail. It is an envelope. Because we are all (well, at least the readers of this book, I hope) are computer users, we have heard of email. So, we immediately connect the envelope with the idea "I can send/receive email with it." Maybe. But what if letters are sent in a totally different way in my culture? They could be rolls or artistically folded sheets. The meaning if the icon becomes completely unclear. Maybe drums or smoke signals would be good symbols for email.

Consider this simple example and you will see how it can mislead us. A diagonal line from the lower left corner to the upper right corner means "upward." Am I right or not? In western culture, this might be true because we read from the left to the right. If we look at this line from the left to the right, it will go upward. We have been conditioned from childhood to think of it as "normal." In other cultures that read from the right to the left, however, this line is going "downward," and is just as "normal." Someone recently asked me, "And if we add an arrow to the top?" A reader reading from the right to the left would probably associate it with "backward."

The diagonal line is a very raw example. In most of the cases, the difference between the imagination and association of icons and other graphics is much more subtle. The University of Namibia conducted an experiment related to icons and signs with the students, and ended up with surprising results. A good example was the No Smoking sign. We all know it: a red circle with a red diagonal on a white background and a cigarette. Everyone knew that it had something to do with smoking, but they weren't so sure about the rest of the sign. An interesting answer was, "Only half cigarettes are allowed to be smoked—but this is nonsense!" The person knew that it didn't make any sense, but it was what she thought.

I'm not suggesting that you not use icons. I'm just emphasizing that not all symbols are intuitively understood worldwide. Intuition comes from the culture(s) in which persons grow up or otherwise become familiar with. This means that in some cultures your icons may not make any sense (in a best-case scenario) or that they are interpreted as something totally different from what you intend (worst-case scenario). Conclusion: Don't depend totally on graphics in your program.

12 Helpers

So far, we've done everything "by hand." It was necessary to understand how KDE works and where problems can come up. KDE offers the programmer tools, however, to hopefully ease the programmer's life. This chapter discusses exactly what those tools are.

12.1 Integrated Development Environments

Integrated Development Environments are not everyone's cup of tea, at least not under UNIX. Emacs users swear that nobody needs anything else. Vim fans back them up and say the same about Vim. The reality is, for those of us who don't sleep with their keyboard, IDEs are a real blessing: They perform a lot of small work for us (generating correct Makefiles, for example).

KDE exists because so many different applications relate to it, making it easy (well, easy enough) for programmers to develop their goods. Qt and KDE provide an excellent "application framework" that enable developers to write appealing programs with a small amount of code. IDEs take care of the "little things."

12.1.1 KDevelop

At the time of this writing, KDevelop is available in the version 1.0beta3. Although, the KDevelop developers claim that the program is still in the beta state, it is already perfectly usable to develop applications with it. Figure 12.1 shows the main window of KDevelop. You can get it at `www.kdevelop.org/`. This site has the latest news, including the current developers' plans.

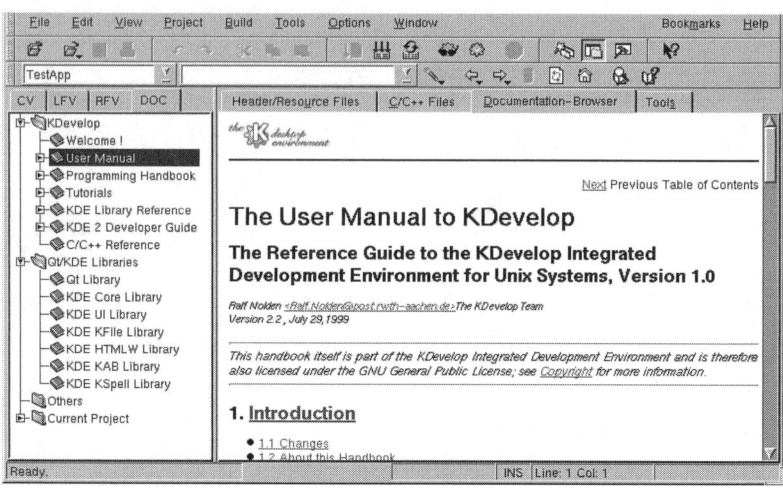

Figure 12.1 *The main window of KDevelop.*

After you have compiled and installed KDevelop over the standard sequence

```
./configure
make
make install
```

the corresponding item will be shown in the panel menu Application. The program will continue its installation with the first execution. It creates the API documentation for the KDE libraries, in a very similar style to the Qt documentation. This documentation as well as Qt's can be displayed within KDevelop just as within kfm or kdehelp. To create it, you have to install the sources of the libraries.

If you create a new project via Project, KAppWizard, then KDevelop will ask you a bunch of questions such as your name, where the project should be created, and so on. Next, the IDE will create a small but completed program including the sources, Makefiles, `*.kdelnk` file, a rudimentary handbook, a README file, and the installation instructions. You can compile this program and execute it. It can't do very much (just like our first version of KTsp), but it's a good starting point for our project.

The left part of the main window of KDevelop contains three different viewers. The right part contains editors for header and source files, just like browsers for different documentation. CV in the left part stands for Class Viewer. It shows all the declared classes and structures of the project in the form of a tree. A click on the plus sign (+) in front of the class name opens a branch with the methods and member variables of this class. A click on the class itself activates the header editor with the opened file and the class declaration in the right part. A click on a method in the CV activates the source editor with the opened file and the definitions in the right part. The cursor is already at the beginning of the implementation of this method. A click on a member variable in the CV displays the header editor in the right part; the cursor is next to the declaration of the variable.

LFV, in the left part means Logical File Viewer. It doesn't group the files after directories, but logical groups such as Header, Sources, GNU, and Others. You can add new groups by right-clicking on the project name at the top of LFV, and then on New LFV Group. Clicking on a file in the LFV activates the editor with the file in the right part.

The RFV in the left part shows the files of the project after the classical way, as a tree of the directories and files. The same here: Clicking on a file activates the editor with the corresponding file in the right part.

All in all, the interaction of the viewers on the left part and the editors on the right part are well thought out. You will appreciate having everything at hand after a short period of working with KDevelop.

There's only DOC left for the documentation at the left side. This viewer shows the documentation for Qt, KDE, and the entire current project. Additionally, you'll get documentation relating to KDevelop itself and an item for all projects developed with KDevelop. A click in the items activates the corresponding documentation.

There are tools in the right part, too.

KDevelop is already a full-blown IDE for fast software development. It really shows what it can do if you install the following three programs (which work very closely together):

- KIconEdit
- KDbg
- KTranslator

KIconEdit is, as I mentioned in the preceding chapter, a tool to create icons corresponding to the KDE standard. It belongs to the official release of KDE, so it should be installed on your system. If you click on an icon in RFV on the left side, Tools will pop up at the right and start KIconEdit with an opened icon. You don't have to leave KDevelop to draw icons for your program.

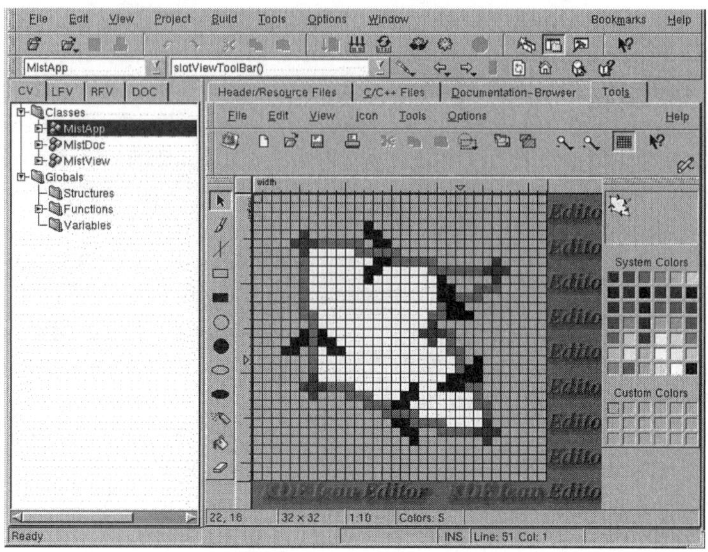

Figure 12.2 *KDevelop with KIconEdit and an opened icon for KTsp.*

KDbg is a KDE-compatible front end for the GNU debugger. KDbg isn't part of the official release, yet. You'll have to download it, compile it, and install it on your own. The URL of the home page of KDbg is

```
http://members.telecom.at/~johsixt/kdbg.html
```

It provides tips and tricks about the usage of KDbg in its most updated version.

Figure 12.3 shows KDevelop with KDbg. The program stopped at a breakpoint. The backtrace can be seen just as the content of the variable. Because KDbg uses `gdb` as the back end, it inherits the skills, too. Its integration into KDevelop is definitely a significant advancement of KDevelop, which you should definitely take a look at. Even if you're not a friend of IDEs, it's still worth downloading KDbg for standalone usage.

Finally, KDevelop can work together with KTranslator, too, as you can see in Figure 12.4. KTranslator helps with the translation of the text into the different languages within your project. The program is part of the package kdesdk, which does not belong to the official releases of KDE. You can download it from `ftp://ftp.kde.org/pub/kde/`. If you aren't considering translating your program to at least one other language, it won't be of interest to you.

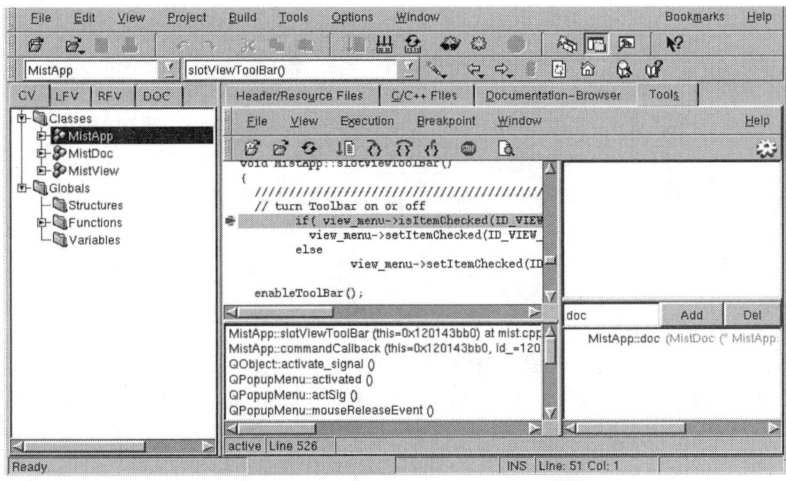

Figure 12.3 *KDevelop with KDbg.*

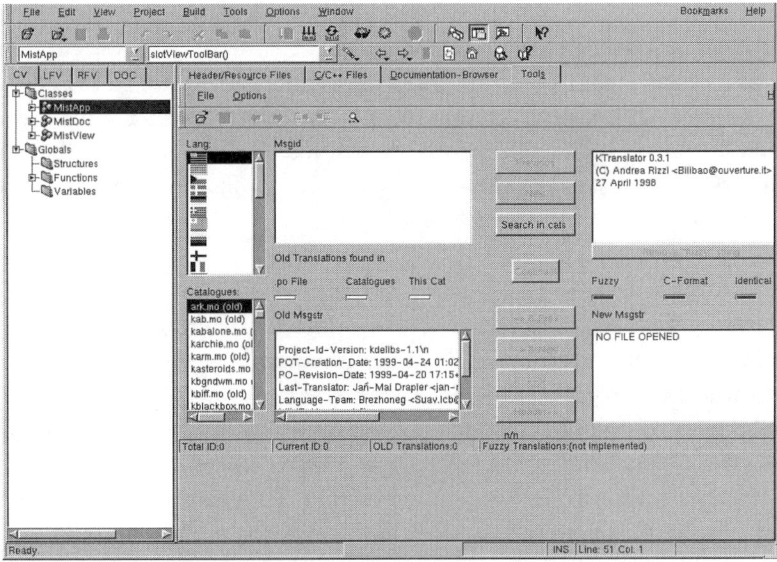

Figure 12.4 *KDevelop with KTranslator.*

This description of KDevelop cannot and is not meant to replace the KDevelop handbook. A full description of KDevelop's functions is way beyond the scope of this book. I do want to encourage you to take a look at the program, however, despite the low version number.

A final thing that you should remember about KDevelop is that it needs the dkoc program (from kdesdk) to create both your program's documentation and the documentation for the KDE libraries. For the creation of the indices of all documentation you'll need `glimse`, too, which should be part of every Linux distribution. Although the documentation can be used without an index, you can't let KDevelop search in it.

12.1.2 KodeKnight

KodeKnight is the second IDE developed for KDE. A lot of information isn't available about it at the moment. KodeKnight is based on CORBA. This makes the IDE a good candidate for KDE 2.0, the next "main version" of KDE, which is supposed to be released at the beginning of 2000. KodeKnight is mentioned here so that you will know that there are other alternatives, especially in KDE 2.0.

12.2 Application Generators

As I previously mentioned, not all programmers like IDEs. This is especially true of many UNIX programmers. If you belong to these Emacs- or Vim-addicted crowd, you would probably still like to have a whole "application framework" generated as the starting point. Application generators take care of that for you.

12.2.1 KAppgen

KAppgen generates all needed files for a minimal KDE application doing nothing more than displaying itself onscreen and terminating. It's a good start for a new project.

KAppgen belongs to the package kdesdk, which can be downloaded from the KDE's FTP address. After you've compiled and installed KAppgen, you can find the program under the panel menu Applications. If you execute KAppgen, you'll be presented with four pages of questions about your new project. You must answer these questions. Figure 12.5 shows the first one of these pages. After you've finished everything, choose File, Generate Application. KAppgen will generate the project with all the needed files. Now you can start to develop your program with the tool of your choice.

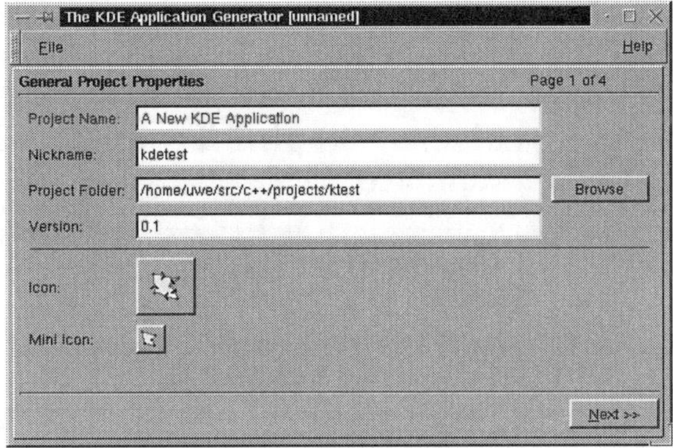

Figure 12.5 *The first page of KAppgen.*

12.2.2 Shaman

Shaman is actually a lot more than an application generator for KDE. It likes to describe itself as a system for generating documents. The files needed for a KDE project are also documents and that's why we'll use Shaman as a generator for "application frameworks." The program has a Web site:

```
www.kirchheim.netsurf.de/~tfischer/shaman.html
```

You can get the program itself and information about new developments from this site.

After you have installed Shaman, a new item will appear on the panel menu: Developer. You can execute the program with it presenting itself as in Figure 12.6. In the left part of the main window of Shaman, you'll see the directory tree with the already existing document templates. There are three document templates for KDE:

- Minimal
- Standard
- KOffice\index{KOffice}

A minimal KDE application is a program with a main window without a menu, toolbar, and statusbar. A standard application has a menubar and a toolbar. The KOffice template generates an application for KOffice, KDE's office applications. The standard template is good for most of the programs. If you choose a template in the left part of the window, Shaman will display information about it in the right part. If you're pleased with it, you can start the generator by clicking on File, New Project from Template.

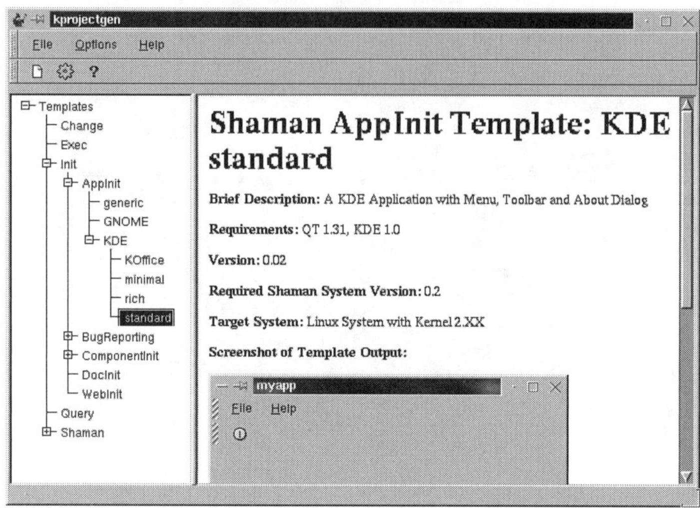

Figure 12.6 *Shaman generates a KDE application.*

13

Becoming a Part of KDE

KDE is more than just another freeware project. KDE is an international team of programmers creating the new standard desktop for UNIX in general and Linux in particular. What began as a small group of undaunted people is now a worldwide band of programmers, system administrators, artists, translators, and users.

As you might already think, such a diverse group creates problems. Artists see things differently than programmers most of the time; translators need other time frames for their work than the programmers who want to release their code as fast as possible. The creators of KDE came from different cultures. Sometimes communication hits rough patches when someone understands something as rude, although the other one didn't mean it that way.

The diversity of the personalities and cultures, which come together in KDE, provides a big advantage going far beyond a technical advantage. Those who actively take part in KDE make new friends from totally different cultural backgrounds and surroundings. Not all communication is about technical questions, although it is in the foreground.

Naturally, every programmer can take part in developing applications without taking part in the discussions about KDE. No one will force you to become a part of the community. If you don't, however, you'll lose the possibility to influence the further development of KDE or to get help.

13.1 The Mailing Lists

The mailing lists are the cornerstone of the communication possibilities of KDE. They're listed under `www.kde.org/contact.html`. The most important list for programmers is `kde-devel@kde.org`. Hundreds of developers discuss their projects, their difficulties, and their strategies on this list. You can find an archive of all KDE-related lists at `http://lists.kde.org`.

The spectrum goes from "Why doesn't the following piece of code compile correctly?" to "The class XY wastes tons of memory!", and to "Here's a design for our interface to databases." Especially for programmers who write their first project, this list is an inexhaustible treasure chest. Before you ask a question that's already been asked 199 times, you should take a look in the lists' archives to see whether or not you can find the answer there.

The language of all lists is English, although most people don't speak English as their native language. Please keep this in mind. If it seems that somebody is rude, please remember the language differences. The "rudeness" might just be a misunderstanding, without a slight ever being intended.

You can sign up for this list by sending an email to `kde-devel-request@kde.org` with "subscribe joe@mydomain"[1] on the subject line. Because this information might have changed since the time of this writing, it's always better to take a look at the Web site for any updated information. Shortly after we get your email address, you'll receive the first mailing from the list. Please abstain from asking user questions on `kde-devel@kde.org`. This list is for developers. Users have other lists from which they can ask things like "How do I configure my panel so that it's not at the bottom?"

There're special lists for big projects like KOffice. If you want to work on these projects, you should sign up for the corresponding lists. The Web site names all the lists and is more current than this book.

13.2 The Newsgroups

Two KDE newsgroups exist, a German one and an international (English) one:

- de.alt.comp.kde
- comp.windows.x.kde

Users are the majority participants in these newsgroups, but programmers also find them interesting. Programmers often answer user questions through the newsgroups, and also find feedback from other users regarding various problems, including misunderstood functions. These responses are useful because users have another understanding of "easy to use" than programmers do. If you don't just want to read, but also to post answers, you should stick to the corresponding language.

[1] *Of course, you have to replace this email address with your own.*

A new newsgroup specific to KDE development is being discussed. It would be located at `comp.windows.x.kde-devel` or something similar (check the Web site). Because setting up a newsgroup involves a lot of work and voting in the Usenet (the "newsgroup part" of the Internet), I can't say right now how soon this new newsgroup might become available. If you come across a vote on this issue while perusing the KDE mailing lists, please take part.

13.3 The IRC Channel

For fast communication without the delay of email, you can use the Internet Relay Chat (IRC) channel for KDE on the server `irc.kde.org`. The channel is `#kde`. Most of the time, the mailing lists offer the better way to communicate because of the different time zones around the globe. Sometimes you need a fast response, however, and that's what the channel is for.

13.4 CVS

An introduction to the Concurrent Versions System (CVS) would go far beyond the scope of this book. CVS is a system to save different versions of documents in a central repository. It is an additional layer to the well-known Revision Control System (RCS) and provides methods to solve conflict created by many developers working on the same source.

The complete code for all libraries and applications in the official releases of KDE and of some other applications can be found in a CVS Repository on the server `cvs.kde.org`. As long as you're writing a program for KDE only, you don't need to bother with CVS. If you work on the base of KDE, or on the Killer-Application that everyone wants to have and needs to become a part of the official releases of KDE, you'll need access to the CVS server. Stephan Kulow (`coolo@kde.org`) is the coordinator of this server. He's the one to contact if you need full access to this server. My hint: First, start to program for KDE. CVS has time.

13.5 FTP

The software needs to get to the users. Besides the CDs of the Linux distributions, this is mainly done by downloading it from FTP servers. Numerous servers around the world distribute the load. The Web site `www.kde.org/mirrors.html` provides information about these servers.

If you have decided to release a version of your KDE program, it has to be uploaded to this network of servers. The corresponding server is `upload.kde.org`. To keep the usage at a low level, this is not a download server.

Load your software via FTP to `upload.kde.org/pub/kde/Incoming`. It will be copied to the correct directory over a semi-automatic process. It works only if you've uploaded a correct LSM file[2] A current template for a correct LSM file can be found under `ftp://ftp.kde.org/pub/kde/Incoming/00LSM.README`. It might appear to be complicated, but it's necessary for the semi-automatic copy process. If you have doubts about some of the fields in the LSM file, take a look at some of the other LSM files. It's important that you fill out the Primary Site line very carefully and specify where your program should be copied. You can direct your questions to `ftpmaster@kde.org`.

When everything is finished, your package will be copied and distributed over the other FTP servers. How long it takes depends on the workload on `upload.kde.org`. If the distribution of the package begins, the server will generate an announcement from your LSM file and send it to the mailing list `kde-announce@kde.org`.

[2] *LSM stands for Linux Software Map.*

14

The Future of KDE

The future has already started. While programmers, artists, and translators prepare KDE 1.1.2,[1] the development of KDE 2.0 is already in the works. The enormous success of KDE has actually accelerated the development of KDE and not slowed it down. Many things will change in KDE, including even the basic technology. (How radical!)

14.1 KOM

The K Object Model/OpenParts (KOM/OP) is a component layer over the Common Object Request Broker Architecture (CORBA). This object model is not new in the sense that it's being developed for KDE 2.0. KOffice has been based on it for more than a year now, and after intensive development and testing, it's time to change KDE to the new technology.

KDE won't consist of single applications, but more so of single components that can be built together into an application. Let's say that KMail reads an email with an MP3 attachment. The current technology gives KMail three possibilities:

1. It can ignore it or ask whether it should be saved.
2. It can be linked with a library being able to deal with MP3 files and play the data with this library.
3. It can start an MP3 player and pass the data to it.

While the first possibility is more like "I can't deal with this," 2 and 3 are very inflexible. In the second case, KMail—or better yet, the developers—would have to know all possible kinds of data that could occur in mail attachments and link the program against an unreasonable number of

[1] *Only bug fixes, more translations, and more new colorful icons for modern graphic cards.*

libraries. In the third case, KMail has to know about the MP3 players installed on the system.

The solution is much easier with CORBA and KOM/OP. KMail notices via mimetypes that the data is of the type MP3, and therefore needs an MP3 player. It requests the service of such a player from the KDE-Trader. The corresponding player (if there is one) will be started, embedded in KMail, and will play the data. From the user's view, it looks like the player is a part of KMail, although in reality it's a totally different application or component.

This approach leads to significantly better flexibility than the current technology. At the time when the program is being compiled and linked, it doesn't need to know about the services it has to provide. Actually, this type of service doesn't even have to exist at this point. All that is needed is one or more methods to determine the service type, and a method that asks the KDE-Trader for such a service. On the other hand, every component that provides a service must register it at the Trader. A picture viewer will register itself with the Trader like this: "I can display JPEG." Then every other component can request this service. Because the registration of a service is done at the installation, services from the offering component (which isn't running) can be used as well.

If this method is used correctly, it not only leads to greater flexibility, but also to smaller applications because properties can be distributed over other components.

14.2 KOffice

KOffice is a new suite of office applications that range from a word processor (KWord) to a spreadsheet application (KSpread) to a vector graphics program (KIllustrator). KOM/OP has been developed parallel to KOffice. KOffice uses this technology more than all the other programs in KDE do.

Every single KOffice application is an OpenPart and can embed all the other ones as well as be embedded in them. Although all the programs that make up KOffice are powerful applications by themselves, their real strength comes from working together. If you take a look at `http://KOffice.kde.org`, you'll see the high level at which KOffice is already and how much KDE stands to gain through KOM/OP.

The single components of KOffice are as follows:

- KWord Word processor
- KSpread Spreadsheet application
- Katabase Database
- KPresenter Graphics presentations

- KIllustrator Vector graphics program
- KFormula Formula editor
- KDiagram Create diagrams
- KImage Display pictures

Although some of these parts of KOffice are still in their preliminary stages, other ones such as KWord, KSpread, and KPresenter are already advanced, but still unsuitable for end users at the time of this writing.

All KOffice programs use the standard XML file format. This way, they avoid the obscure and mostly proprietary file formats and head into a future of open standards. A filter manager for import and export filters for other formats already exists.

14.3 When Is KDE 2.0 Going To Be Released?

Just as with all freeware projects, it's hard to answer this question. The development is going very fast, but something like the complete Office suite isn't produced overnight. Because KDE is based on a completely new technology, it will have to go through long beta cycles.

KDE's plan is to start with the beta cycles in the last quarter of 1999 and to release the final KDE 2.0 and KOffice 1.0 in the first half of the year 2000. Unlike the programmers of commercial software, freeware developers don't have marketing deadlines. The software gets released when it is finished.

Those who want to develop stable applications based on a reliable desktop must trust KDE 1.x, which will stay the standard desktop of Linux for quite a while to come.

The actual dispute—whether the computer desktop will remain hostage to the monopoly of proprietary software—won't really begin before KDE 2.0 is released.

Index

Symbols

A

B

C

D

E

F

G

H

I-J

K

L

M

N

O-P

Q

R

S

T

U

V

W

X-Z

Books for Technology Professionals

Windows NT Thin Client Solutions

by Todd Mathers and Shawn Genoway
1st Edition
$35.00
ISBN: 1-57870-065-5

Explore the cost-saving features of Windows Based Terminal Server—which allows applications to be run on a server—as well as the software based upon Citrix's core ICA (Independent Computing Architecture) protocol which provides enterprise capability.

Windows NT Win32 Perl Programming: The Standard Extensions

by Dave Roth
1st Edition
$40.00
ISBN: 1-57870-067-1

See numerous proven examples and practical uses of Perl in solving everyday Win32 problems. This is the only book available with comprehensive coverage of Win32 extensions, where most of the Perl functionality resides in Windows settings.

Windows NT Domain Architecture

by Gregg Branham
1st Edition
$38.00
ISBN: 1-57870-112-0

As Windows NT continues to be deployed more and more in the enterprise, the domain architecture for the network becomes more critical as the complexity increases. This book contains the in-depth expertise that is necessary to truly plan a complex enterprise domain.

Windows 2000 Server: Planning and Migration

by Sean Deuby
1st Edition
$40.00
ISBN: 1-57870-023-X

Windows 2000 Server: Planning and Migration can quickly save the NT professional thousands of dollars and hundreds of hours. This title includes authoritative information on key features of Windows 2000 and offers recommendations on how to best position your NT network for Windows 2000.

Windows 2000 Quality of Service

by David Iseminger
1st Edition
$45.00
ISBN: 1-57870-115-5

As the traffic on networks continues to increase, the strain on network infrastructure and available resources has also grown. Windows 2000 Quality of Service teaches network engineers and administrators how to define traffic control patterns and utilize bandwidth and their networks.

Windows NT Applications: Measuring and Optimizing Performance

by Paul Hinsberg
1st Edition
$45.00
ISBN: 1-57870-176-7

This book offers developers crucial insight into the underlying structure of Windows NT, as well as the methodology and tools for measuring and ultimately optimizing code performance.

Windows 2000 and Mainframe Integration

by William Zack
1st Edition
$39.99
ISBN: 1-57870-200-3

Windows 2000 and Mainframe Integration provides mainframe computing professionals with the practical know-how to build and integrate Windows 2000 technologies into their current environment.

Windows Script Host

by Tim Hill
1st Edition
$35.00
ISBN: 1-57870-139-2

Windows Script Host is one of the first books published about this powerful tool. The text focuses on system scripting and the VBScript language, using objects, server scriptlets, and ready to use script solutions.

Programming

Handbook of Programming Languages, Volume I

Edited by Peter Salus
1st Edition
$49.99
ISBN: 1-57870-008-6

This is the most comprehensive source on the principal object-oriented languages. It covers languages from Smalltalk to Java, with explanations of the languages' histories, descriptions of their syntax and semantics, how-to information and tips, and pointers to potential traps.

Handbook of Programming Languages, Volume II

Edited by Peter Salus
1st Edition
$49.99
ISBN: 1-57870-009-4

The four most important imperative languages are covered in this title: Fortran, C, Turbo Pascal, and Icon. Evaluate them to find the best imperative language for your purpose at hand, and learn how these languages are related to each other historically and syntactically.

Handbook of Programming Languages, Volume III

Edited by Peter Salus
1st Edition
$49.99
ISBN: 1-57870-010-8

Beginning with Jon Bentley's discussion of little languages, this book continues to discuss languages "specialized to a particular problem domain"—such as Perl, sed, awk, SQL, Tcl/Tk, Python and more.

Handbook of Programming Languages, Volume IV

Edited by Peter Salus
1st Edition
$49.99
ISBN: 1-57870-011-6

This book begins with the functional programming group, descended from John McCarthy's LISP of the late 1960s, and moves on to discuss its offspring: Emacs Lisp, Scheme, Guile and CLOS.

Smart Card Developers Kit
by Scott Guthery and Tim Jurgensen)
1st Edition
$79.99
ISBN: 1-57870-027-2

This is all the practical information a computing professional needs to write programs that use and run on smart cards. Smart card communications and commands, SDKs, terminal-side and card-side APIs, security, financial applications and e-commerce are all covered in this title.

DCE/RPC over SMB
by Luke Leighton
1st Edition
$45.00
ISBN: 1-57870-150-3

Security people, system and network administrators, and the folks writing tools for them all need to be familiar with the packets flowing across their networks. Authored by a key member of the SAMBA team, this book describes how Microsoft has taken DCE/RPC and implemented it over SMB and TCP/IP.

Autoconf, Automake, and Libtool
by Ben Elliston, et al.
1st Edition
$34.99, Spring 2000
ISBN: 1-57870-190-2

This book is the first of its kind, authored by Open Source community luminaries and current maintainers of the tools, teaching developers how to boost their productivity and the portability of their applications using GNU autoconf, GNU automake and GNU libtool.

Delphi COM Programming
by Eric Harmon
1st Edition
$45.00, Winter 2000
ISBN: 1-57870-221-6

Delphi COM Programming is for all Delphi 4 and 5 programmers. After providing readers with an understanding of the COM framework, it offers a practical exploration of COM to enable Delphi developers to program component-based applications. Typical real-world scenarios, such as Windows Shell programming, automating Microsoft Agent, and creating and using ActiveX controls, are explored. Discussions of each topic are illustrated with detailed examples.

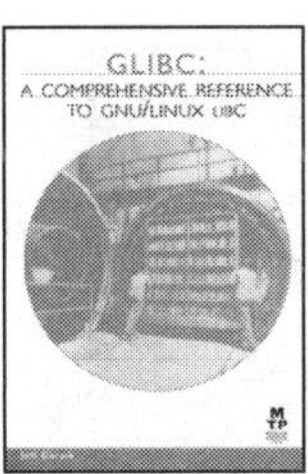

glibc: A Comprehensive Reference to GNU/Linux libC

by Jeff Garzik
1st Edition
$40.00, Winter 2000
ISBN: 1-57870-202-X

glibc: A Comprehensive Reference to GNU/Linux libC comprises over 1,800 functions. A complete reference work — encompassing a single-volume version that gives quick coverage to each function. It includes an easily-searched index to provide added value. The book content consists of an index of functions by category (networking, threading, string, etc), and then an alphabetical function listing.

Networking

LDAP: Programming Directory Enabled Applications

by Tim Howes and Mark Smith
$44.99
ISBN: 1-57870-000-0

This overview of the LDAP standard discusses its creation and history with the Internet Engineering Task Force, as well as the original RFC standard. LDAP also covers compliance trends, implementation, data packet handling in C++, client/server responsibilities and more.

ASDL/VSDL Principles

by Dennis Rushmayer
1st Edition
$44.99
ISBN: 1-57870-015-9

ASDL/VSDL Principles provides the communications and networking engineer with the practical explanations, technical detail, and in-depth insight needed to fully implement ASDL and VDSL. Coverage includes the fundamentals of the transmission theory and crosstalk in the outside plant, including the details of modeling and simulating the expected performance of ADSL and VDSL under different operating conditions.

DSL: Specialization Techniques and Standards

by Walter Chen
1st Edition
$54.99
ISBN: 1-57870-017-5

DSL is ideal for computing professionals who are looking for information on new high-speed communications technologies, and information on the dynamics of ADSL communications in order to create compliant applications. Get calculation examples for all signal environments, and coverage of ADSL and a multitude of other xDSL technologies.

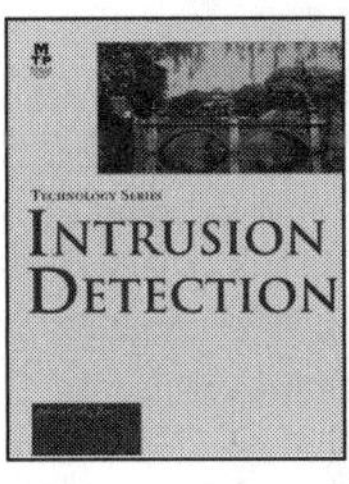

Intrusion Detection

by Rebecca Bace
1st Edition, Winter 2000
$50.00
ISBN: 1-57870-185-6

Intrusion detection is a critical new area of technology within network security. This comprehensive guide to the field of intrusion detection covers the foundations of intrusion detection and system audit. *Intrusion Detection* provides a wealth of information, ranging from design considerations and how to evaluate and choose the optimal commercial intrusion detection products for a particular networking environment.

Designing Addressing Architectures for Routing and Switching

by Howard Berkowitz
1st Edition
$45.00
ISBN: 1-57870-059-0

One of the greatest challenges for a network design professional is making visible the users, servers, files, printers and other resources on their network. This title equips the network engineer or architect with a systematic methodology for planning the wide area and local area network "streets" on which users and servers live.

Understanding & Deploying LDAP Directory Services

by Tim Howes; Mark Smith; Gordon Good
1st Edition
$50.00
ISBN: 1-57870-070-1

This comprehensive tutorial provides the reader with a thorough treatment of LDAP directory services. Minimal knowledge of general networking and administration is assumed, making the material accessible to intermediate and advanced readers alike. The text is full of practical implementation advice and real-world deployment examples to help the reader choose the path that makes the most sense for the specific organization.

Switched, Fast and Gigabit Ethernet, Third Edition

by Sean Riley and Robert Breyer
3rd Edition
$39.99
ISBN: 1-57870-073-6

Switched, Fast, and Gigabit Ethernet, Third Edition is the one and only solution needed to understand and fully implement this entire range of Ethernet innovations. Acting as both an overview of current technologies and hardware requirements as well as a hands-on, comprehensive tutorial for deploying and managing switched, fast, and gigabit ethernet networks, this guide covers the most prominent present and future challenges network administrators face.

Wireless LANs: Implementing Interoperable Networks
by Jim Geier
1st Edition
$40.00
ISBN: 1-57870-081-7

Wireless LANs covers how and why to migrate from proprietary solutions to the 802.11 standard, and explains how to realize significant cost savings through wireless LAN implementation for data collection systems.

Wide Area High Speed Networks
by Dr. Sidnie Feit
1st Edition
$50.00
ISBN: 1-57870-114-7

Networking is in a transitional phase between long-standing conventional wide area services and new technologies and services. This book presents current and emerging wide area technologies and services, makes them understandable, and puts them into perspective so that their merits and disadvantages are clear.

The DHCP Handbook
by Ralph Droms
and Ted Lemon
1st Edition
$50.00
ISBN: 1-57870-137-6

The DHCP Handbook is an authoritative overview and expert guide to the set up and management of a DHCP server. This title discusses how DHCP was developed and its interaction with other protocols. Also, learn how DHCP operates, its use in different environments, and the interaction between DHCP servers and clients. Network hardware, inter-server communication, security, SNMP, and IP mobility are also discussed. Included in the book are several appendices that provide a rich resource for networking professionals working with DHCP.

Designing Routing and Switching Architectures for Enterprise Networks
by Howard Berkowitz
1st Edition
$45.00
ISBN: 1-57870-060-4

This title provides a fundamental understanding of how switches and routers operate, enabling the reader to effectively use them to build networks. The book walks the network designer through all aspects of requirements, analysis and deployment strategies, strengthens reader's professional abilities, and helps them develop skills necessary to advance in their profession.

Software Architecture and Engineering

Designing Flexible Object-Oriented Systems with UML
by Charles Richter
1st Edition
$40.00
ISBN: 1-57870-098-1

Designing Flexible Object-Oriented Systems with UML details the UML, which is a notation system for designing object-oriented programs. The book follows the same sequence that a development project might employ, starting with requirements of the problem using UML use case diagrams and activity diagrams. The reader is shown ways to improve the design as the author moves through the transformation of the initial diagrams into class diagrams and interaction diagrams. The author continues offering tips and strategies for improving the design and ultimately incorporating concurrency, distribution, and persistence into the design example.

Constructing Superior Software

Paul Clements, et al
1st Edition
$40.00
ISBN: 1-57870-147-3

This title presents a set of fundamental engineering strategies for achieving a successful software solution, with practical advice to ensure that the development project is moving in the right direction. Software designers and development managers can improve the development speed and quality of their software, and improve the processes used in development.

A UML Pattern Language

by Paul Evitts
1st Edition
$45.00, Winter 2000
ISBN: 1-57870-118-X

While other books focus only on the UML notation system, this book integrates key UML modeling concepts and illustrates their use through patterns. It provides an integrated, practical, step-by-step discussion of UML patterns, with real-world examples to illustrate proven software modeling techniques.

New Riders

How to Contact Us

Visit Our Web Site

www.newriders.com

On our Web site, you'll find information about our other books, authors, tables of contents, indexes, and book errata. You can also place orders for books through our Web site.

Email Us

Contact us at this address:

newriders@mcp.com

- If you have comments or questions about this book
- To report errors that you have found in this book
- If you have a book proposal to submit or are interested in writing for New Riders
- If you would like to have an author kit sent to you
- If you are an expert in a computer topic or technology and are interested in being a technical editor who reviews manuscripts for technical accuracy

newriders@mcp.com

- To find a distributor in your area, please contact our international department at the address above.

nrmedia@mcp.com

- For instructors from educational institutions who wish to preview New Riders books for classroom use. Email should include your name, title, school, department, address, phone number, office days/hours, text in use, and enrollment in the body of your text along with your request for desk/examination copies and/or additional information.

Write to Us

New Riders Publishing
201 W. 103rd St.
Indianapolis, IN 46290-1097

Call Us

Toll-free (800) 571-5840 + 9 + 7424
If outside U.S. (317) 581-3500. Ask for New Riders.

Fax Us

(317) 581-4663

New Riders

We Want to Know What You Think

To better serve you, we would like your opinion on the content and quality of this book. Please complete this card and mail it to us or fax it to 317-581-4663.

Name______________________________

Address ______________________________

City ____________________State ______Zip __________

Phone ______________________________

Email Address ______________________________

Occupation ______________________________

Operating System(s) that you use ______________________________

What influenced your purchase of this book?

- ❑ Recommendation ❑ Cover Design
- ❑ Table of Contents ❑ Index
- ❑ Magazine Review ❑ Advertisement
- ❑ New Riders' Reputation ❑ Author Name

How would you rate the contents of this book?

- ❑ Excellent ❑ Very Good
- ❑ Good ❑ Fair
- ❑ Below Average ❑ Poor

How do you plan to use this book?

- ❑ Quick reference ❑ Self-training
- ❑ Classroom ❑ Other

What do you like most about this book? Check all that apply.

- ❑ Content ❑ Writing Style
- ❑ Accuracy ❑ Examples
- ❑ Listings ❑ Design
- ❑ Index ❑ Page Count
- ❑ Price ❑ Illustrations

What do you like least about this book? Check all that apply.

- ❑ Content ❑ Writing Style
- ❑ Accuracy ❑ Examples
- ❑ Listings ❑ Design
- ❑ Index ❑ Page Count
- ❑ Price ❑ Illustrations

What would be a useful follow-up book to this one for you? ____________________

Where did you purchase this book? ____________________

Can you name a similar book that you like better than this one, or one that is as good? Why?

How many New Riders books do you own? ____________________

What are your favorite computer books? ____________________

What other titles would you like to see us develop? ____________________

Any comments for us?____________________

KDE Application Development, 1-57870-201-1

Fold here and tape to mail

Place
Stamp
Here

New Riders Publishing
201 W. 103rd St.
Indianapolis, IN 46290